Tomasz J. Kopański

Barbar
Victims
Luftwaffe Kills in the East

First published in Poland in 2001 by Robert Pęczkowski
Usługi Informatyczne, Orzeszkowej 2/57, 39-400 Tarnobrzeg, Poland
e-mail: robertp@zt.tarnobrzeg.tpsa.pl
with cooperation of
Mushroom Model Publications,36 Ver Road, Redbourn, AL3 7PE, UK.
e-mail: rogerw@waitrose.com

WYDAWNICTWO DIECEZJALNE SANDOMIERZ

Printed in Poland

ISBN 83-7300-065-8

Editor in chief	Roger Wallsgrove
Editors	Bartłomiej Belcarz
	Robert Pęczkowski
	Artur Juszczak
Edited by	Robert Pęczkowski
Page design by	Artur Juszczak
	Robert Pęczkowski
Cover Layout	Artur Juszczak
DTP	Artur Juszczak
Translation	Robert Pęczkowski
	& Roger Wallsgrove
Proofreading	Roger Wallsgrove
	Roman Postek
Colour Profiles	Witold Hazuka
	Artur Juszczak
Printed by	Drukarnia Diecezjalna Sandomierz
Photos:	Tomasz J. Kopański coll. except where stated

Table of Contents:

Acknowledgements

B. Belcarz

M. Bukhman

K. Cieślak

F. Gerdessen

A. Juszczak

W. Matusiak

K. H. Münch

P. Petrick

R. Pęczkowski

M. Wawrzyński

T. E. Willis

**Special thanks for great help for my best
friend Robert Michulec.**

Selected Bibliography

* Alyeksyenko Vasyliy, Sovetskye VVS Nakanunye in: Gody Vyelikoy Otyechestvyennoy Voyny, part 1-4, in: Aviatsya i Kosmonautika 2000, No 1 - 4.
* Anderson Lennart, Soviet Aircraft and Aviation 1917-1941, London, Putnam 1994
* Arsyenyev Evgeniy, Samolety OKB im. A. I. Mikoyana. MiG-1, in: Aviatsya i Kosmonautika 2000, No 4.
* Batailes Aeriennes No 12 and No 13: Operation Barbarossa part 1 and part 2.
* Belcarz Bartłomiej, Pęczkowski Robert, Gloster Gladiator, Gdynia, AJ-Press, 1996
* Bergström Christer, Mikhailov Andrey, Black Cross / Red Star. Air War Over the Eastern Front. Vol. I: Operation Barbarossa 1941, Pacifica Military History, Pacifica, California, 2000.
* Bock Robert, Sowieckie Lotnictwo Morskie 1941-1945, Gdynia, AJ-Press, 1996.
* Bock Robert, Jak-1. Jak-3, Gdynia, AJ-Press, 1998.
* Chazanov Dimitriy, Gordyukov Nikolay, Blizniy Bombardirovchik Su-2, Moskva 2000.
* Gamziukas Algirdas, Ramoška Gytis, Lietuvos Karine Aviacija 1919-1940, Kaunas 1999.
* Irbitis Karlis, Of Struggle and Flight. The History of Latvian Aviation, Stittsville, Ontario, Canada's Wings, 1986.
* Kulikov Victor, Moshchanskiy Ilya, Opieracya Barbarossa. Vozdushnye Srazheniya 1941 Goda, Moskva 2000.
* Maslov Michail, Istrebitiel I-16, Armada No 2, Moskva 1997.
* Maslov Michail, Pervye 'SB', in: M.Hobby 2000, No 2
* Michulec Robert, Elita Luftwaffe, Gdynia, Armagedon, 1999.
* Michulec Robert, Il-2, Il-10, Gdynia, AJ-Press, 1995.
* Michulec Robert, Odwiedziny Barbarossy, in: Aero-Technika Lotnicza, 1990, No 7.
* Michulec Robert, Stalinowskie Sokoły, Gdynia, AJ-Press, 1995.
* Myedvyed Aleksandr, Chazanov Dimitriy, Petlyakov Pe-2, Part 1, Armada No 13, Moskva 1999.
* Rezmer Waldemar, Litewskie Lotnictwo Wojskowe 1919-1940, Toruń 1999.
* Stapfer Hans-Heiri, Il-2 Stormovik in Action, Carrollton, Texas, Squadron/Signal Publ. 1995.
* Stapfer Hans-Heiri, LaGG Fighters in Action, Carrollton, Texas, Squadron/Signal Publ. 1996.
* Stapfer Hans-Heiri, Polikarpov Fighters in Action Part 1 and Part 2, Carrollton, Texas, Squadron/Signal Publ. 1995/96.
* Stapfer Hans-Heiri, Yak Fighters in Action, Carrollton, Texas, Squadron/Signal Publ. 1986.
* Vanags - Baginskis Alex, Chronicle of the Remarkable ANT-6, in: Air Enthusiast, Thirty-Five.
* Wawrzyński Mirek, Barbarossa w Powietrzu, in: Militaria i Fakty", 2001, No 1-2.

Glossary

AA	- (Armieyskaya Aviatsiya) - Army Aviation
AD	- (Aviatsionnaya Diviziya) - Aviation Division
AE	- (Aviatsionnaya Eskadrilya) - Aviation Squadron
BAB	- (Bombardirovochnaya Aviatsionnaya Brigada) - Bomber Aviation Brigade
BAD	- (Bombardirovochnaya Aviatsionnaya Diviziya) -Bomber Aviation Division
BAK	- (Bombardirovochniy Aviatsionniy Korpus) - Bomber Aviation Corps
BAP	- (Bombardirovochniy Aviatsionniy Polk) - Bomber Aviation Regiment
BBAP	- (Blizhnebombardirovochniy Aviatsionniy Polk) -Short-range Bomber Aviation Regiment
DBA	- (Dal'ne Bombardirovochnaya Aviatsiya) -Long Range Bomber Aviation
DBAD	- (Dal'ne Bombardirovochnaya Aviatsionnaya Diviziya) -Long Range Bomber Aviation Division
DBAP	- (Dal'ny Bombardirovochniy Aviatsionniy Polk) -Long Range Bomber Aviation Regiment
FA	- (Frontovaya Aviatsiaya) - Front aviation; aviation of military districts
IAB	- (Istriebitel'naya Aviatsionnaya Brigada) - Fighter Aviation Brigade
IAD	- (Istriebitel'naya Aviatsionnaya Diviziya) -Fighter Aviation Division
IAP	- (Istriebitel'niy Aviatsionniy Polk) -Fighter Aviation Regiment
JG	- (Jagdgechwader) - Fighter Group
KAE	- (Korpusnaya Aviatsionnaya Eskadrilya) - Aviation Squadron of the Ground Army Corps.
KG	- (Kampfgeschwader) - Bomber Group
MTAP	- (Minno - Torpedniy Aviatsionniy Polk) -Mine - Torpedo Aviation Regiment
OMRAP	- (Otdielniy Morskoy Razvedyvatelniy Aviatsionniy Polk) - Independent Naval Reconnaissance Aviation Regiment
ORAE	- (Otdelnaya Razvedyvatelnaya Aviatsionnaya Eskadrilya) - Independent Reconnaissance Aviation Squadron
PVO	- (Protivo-Vozdushnaya Oborona) - Home Air Defence
RAP	- (Razvedyratelniy Aviatsionniy Polk) - Reconnaissance Aviation Regiment
SAB	- (Smeshannaya Aviatsionnaya Brigada) - Composite Aviation Brigade
SAD	- (Smeshannaya Aviatsionnaya Diviziya) -Composite Aviation Division
SAP	- (Smeshanniy Aviatsionniy Polk) - Composite Aviation Regiment
SBAP	- (Skorostnoy Bombardiriovochniy Aviatsionniy Polk) -High-speed Bomber Aviation Regiment
ShAP	- (Shturmovoy Aviatsionniy Polk) -Ground Attack Aviation Regiment
TBAP	- (Tyazhyeliy Bombardiriovochniy Aviatsionniy Polk) -Heavy Bomber Aviation Regiment
VMF	- (Voyenno Morskoy Flot) - The Navy
VVS	-(Voyenno Vozdushnye Sily) -Military Air Forces

Introduction

At dawn on 22 July 1941 German forces attacked their "best friend" - Stalin's Russia on a long front spanning from the Baltic Sea to the Carpathian Mountains.

The speed and concentration of attacking German forces, panzer and motorized divisions, supported by heavy attacks from the air, allowed them to achieve deep penetration into the territory of the USSR. At the beginning of September 1941, the Germans had reached as far as Leningrad in the north and Kiev in the south, and in October were approaching the very capital of the "Red Empire" - Moscow.

This first stages of war in Russia mark a time of great success for the Luftwaffe, which, as in previous campaigns, was ordered to wipe out the enemy's aviation. On 22 July at 03:15, selected crews of KG 2, KG 3 and KG 53 attacked 31 Russian airfields where Soviet fighter units were based. Soon the subsequent waves of hundreds of German bombers and fighters attacked other airfields: 66 in all; some of them repeatedly. Luftwaffe pilots dropped thousands of SD-2 bombs and strafed Soviet aircraft, lined up as if on parade.

By the end of that day JG 53 had claimed 74 victories in the air and 28 on the ground. Pilots of JG 51 had claimed 69 air victories and 129 aircraft destroyed on the ground, while those of JG 54 claimed 45 and 35 respectively.

Very high scores were also reported by the crews of Zerstörers and bombers. For example, SKG 210 equipped with Bf 110's destroyed 344 aircraft on the ground and another 8 in the air in 13 attacks on 14 airfields. A single Ju 88 of 3./KG 3 Blitz, piloted by Lt. Ihrig, devastated 39 SBAP based at Pinsk airfield. The bomber crew claimed 60 Soviet aircraft had been destroyed on the ground, and the Soviets later confirmed that 43 SB and 5 Pe-2 airplanes had been destroyed. At Kurovice,

Early morning of 22 July 1941. Stunning aerial photos of a Soviet airfield under attack. In the first photo an I-153 with its covers still. Note German SD-2 bombs (in the upper portion of the photo) which proved extremely effective against parked aircraft.

After the attack - at the captured Soviet airfield. Destroyed I-153 fighter with Bf109E, (probably of JG 77), in the background. Under the Messerschmitt's fuselage is a bomb rack for 96 SD-2 bombs. SD-2 bombs were used only during the first days of the German attack.

Another Soviet airfield with wrecks of MiG-3, Yak-4 and I-153.

close to Lwów, Ju 88s of KG 51 destroyed 34 I-153s of 66 ShAP. At Brześć, Bf109s accounted for 65 I-16s of 122 IAP, and finally at Grodno another 41 I-16 and 5 I-153 of 33 IAP also fell their victim.

Units of the Western Special Military District suffered the heaviest losses. According to Soviet data, 9 SAD lost 347 aircraft out of 440, 10 SAD lost 188 out of 239 aircraft, 11 SAD lost 127 of its 199, 43 IAD also lost most of its aircraft. By the end of the day German fliers had claimed a total of 1,811 enemy aircraft destroyed, including 322 in the air. The Germans lost 61 aircraft and 11 were lost by Romanian units. These scores are considered reliable. The Russians published much smaller losses and much higher victories, but admitted that by noon of 22 June they had lost no less than 1,200 aircraft, including 336 in the air.

One has to ask why were the Russians so surprised, and why in the first days of war were their losses so heavy? It seems there were several reasons for this. In 1939-1940, just after signing of the treaty between USSR and Germany, the Russians got hold of a huge part of Central-Eastern Europe: in September 1939 almost 51% of Poland, in March of 1940 (after the "Winter War") the southern part of Finland, and in June 1940 all of Lithuania, Latvia and Estonia. Also parts of Romania, North Bukovina and Besarabia, came under Soviet control.

Remains of Soviet aircraft destroyed by SD-2 bombs. Parked in rows and not camouflaged, Soviet fighters (MiG-1 and I-16 here) were very easy targets for German airmen.

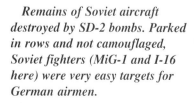

After that "rearrangement" of the borders, the Soviets started to move many military units, including air units, to the newly gained territories. Because Stalin, having 21,000 aircraft and 23,000 tanks at his disposal, planned to attack Germany, many of the new airfields were located extremely close to the new border. In many cases within range of German artillery.

The German attack came at the worst possible time for the Russians. They did not have the time necessary to complete the concentration of their army on the western border, and their aviation units had only just started to re-equip with modern aircraft.

In 1940 Soviet industry delivered 10,565 aircraft, but only 86 of the more modern type. Another batch of modern aircraft could be built as late as March 1941 (see table no. 1), and units only started receiving them in April and May.

The new aircraft were flawed and suffered many failures, especially the MiG-1/MiG-3, and by the time of the German attack, only a small group of pilots could be trained to fly them. As a result, during the German assault on many airfields located in the western part of the country, where the new aircraft had been sent, high numbers of aircraft were present (see table no. 2). Most regiments opted to keep their old aircraft until all pilots could be ready to switch to the new types. A lot of aircraft were stored at the airfields, making them excellent and easy targets for enemy fliers.

Bombs suddenly started to fall on Russian units at dawn on 22 June 1941. Much of the blame for their unpreparedness fell on Stalin, who until the very end refused to believe the intelligence reports about Germany's preparations for the attack. Units were further weakened by Stalin's "purges", ridding them of experienced fliers, since many officers had

I-153 fighters destroyed during air raids.

been murdered or sent to concentration camps in the East. Soviet Aviation, a great power of 61 Air Divisions with 21,000 aircraft (of which 10,000 were based in the western part of Russia), has been incapacitated in the very first days of war, proving its greatness to be purely theoretical (see table 3 and 4).

The first day of war revealed that German units of Luftflotte 1, 2 and 4, with 3,000 aircraft, obtained air superiority easily. It is important to remember, however, that the surprise factor of the attack as well as the destruction of high numbers of Soviet aircraft on the ground, contributed to this success greatly. In spite of this clearly disastrous blow, the Russians still had approximately 8,000 aircraft in airworthy condition left by the end of that day; three times the number of what the Germans could launch. But it is not the number of aircraft alone that is most important in understanding the fiasco of the Soviet Air Force at the beginning of the conflict. The Luftwaffe was superior in almost all aspects. For example, Soviet aviation lacked a unified command. The DBA for instance, which composed 13.5% of the force, went under the Central Commander, while the rest of the aviation: 40.5% under the Military District command, 43.7% under Army command, with the remaining 2.3% under the corps command. Naval

Wreck of an I-16 fighter, abandoned at the edge of airfield, showing the underwing RS-82 rocket rails and a bomb rack.

This MiG-3 from one of the 15 SAD regiments was destroyed by German bombs at the former Polish airfield at Lwów.

Aviation was independent from the Army Air Force. All of this made coordinating any aviation operations almost impossible, contributing considerably to high losses.

German technological advantages were also of importance. Their aircraft were more advanced, faster, better armed and equipped. Typical Russian aircraft sported only a basic set of flying instruments, while radio equipment, especially in fighters, was very rare. Theoretically, every 15th aircraft should have been outfitted with radio gear; mostly the commanders' machines. But among the first 1,000 Yak-1s built, not even one came with a radio. Lack of radio communication in combat aircraft made it difficult to control operations in the air. It should also be noted that many Soviet pilots were sent to combat units after only 8-10 hours of flight training. Obviously, such "well trained" pilots were no match for their experienced German counterparts. Also, in Soviet flying schools pilots were not trained to dog fight, or to fly in bad weather conditions (blind flying).

Soviet losses mounted rapidly as the battle continued. On 23 June the Germans destroyed 755 enemy aircraft; 24 June -

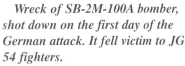

Wreck of SB-2M-100A bomber, shot down on the first day of the German attack. It fell victim to JG 54 fighters.

Photo: Trautloft.

Ar-2 diving bomber destroyed during an air raid.

Line-up of burned-out I-15bis (I-152) at Kaunas (Kovno) airfield.

557; 25th - 251; 26th - 300 and by July 1, they had already eliminated a total of 4,725 aircraft; 1,392 were destroyed in the air, 112 by Flak, and 3,221 on the ground. Many of the Russian aircraft shot down by Germans were SB and DB-3/3F bombers, which were the easy prey. Pilots of JG 51 claimed 57 SB on 24 July; 68 SB on 25 July; 40 DB-3 on the 26th and 113 aircraft (mostly bombers) on the 30th. On 15 July 1941 the commander of JG 51, Oberst Werner Mölders, claimed his 100th and 101st victories. These spectacular victories were largely possible thanks to the Russians themselves. Bombers were sent against German panzer columns unprotected by fighters. As a result, Russian pilots paid the highest price for the lack of co-ordination and the chaotic command. Bomber units were under the Military Districts command while fighter units were mostly commanded by the Army. Their co-operation and co-ordination were marginal.

In the late summer and autumn of 1941 the Soviets were still losing many aircraft. By the end of September the Germans had claimed 14,500 enemy aircraft destroyed, including 5,000 in the air, and by the end of the year this number reached over 20,000. Officially the Russians admitted that 20,159 aircraft had been destroyed, including 16,620 combat aircraft.

The Russian army also suffered badly. By 30 September the Russians had lost 20,500 tanks and 101,000 guns and mortars. Millions of soldiers had been killed or made POWs.

Remains of Soviet aircraft at Mołodeczno air base.

By the end of 1941 2,663,000 Russian soldiers were killed and 3,350,000 had become POWs. German losses were much smaller for this period. Such heavy casualties inflicted on the Red Army did not, however, cause it to collapse (contrary to German hopes).

Soviet industry, thanks largely to prodigious efforts (including those of women and even children), was able to build 5,600 tanks and 7,900 aircraft by the end of 1941 (see table no 1). These were essential to keep the Soviet Army equipped, but the aircraft produced under bad conditions and by unskilled workers were of inferior quality as compared to those from before the war.

The staggering successes gained by the Germans in Russia had not come easily though. Units fighting on the Eastern Front had, by the end of December, lost no fewer than 2,093 aircraft, including 758 bombers, 568 fighters and 170 dive bombers.

On 27 June 1941 the Germans captured 86 aircraft of 8 SAD at Kaunas (Kovno). In the photo are U-2, UTI-4, I-16 and MiG-3.

Wrecks of 15 SAD aircraft at Skniłów airfield, Lwów.

Another 1,362 aircraft were damaged.

Over the course of the next years the Eastern Front was clearly the most important and the most demanding for the Germans. The Russian ability to recover and restore the power of their Red Army was most significant in the ultimate victory over the Nazis.

In the first stages of war in Russia, the Germans not only destroyed a large number of Russian aircraft but also captured hundreds of aircraft intact, abandoned by the VVS. Only a small number of these aircraft were ever used by the Luftwaffe. Those used by some units were mostly training aircraft (like UTI-4) or liaison types.

It is known that Japan and Iraq showed interest in purchasing captured I-16s and UTI-4s. This, however, could not be accomplished due to the later presence of British troops in Iraq and problems involved with transportation to Japan. Only Finland received some Russian aircraft of several different types. The rest of them were stored and eventually destroyed.

Based on a report dated 1 September 1941 from the Commands of Luftflotte 1, 2, and 4, a table has been prepared listing the number of aircraft captured in the first weeks of war (see table no 5). In this table only the aircraft captured by the Germans up to 6 July 1941 are shown, which for example, excludes aircraft captured in both Estonia and eastern Latvia. Because German documents indicated no specific locations, it could only be assumed that aircraft captured by Luftflotte 1 must have been located in Lithuania and Latvia, to the north of the Gołdap-Kovno-Dryssa line. Aircraft captured by Luftflotte 2 were on former Polish territory and Belarus, up to the line of Chełm-Dawidgródek-Mozyr-Homel on the south. Luftflotte 4 found aircraft to the south of that line, i.e. south to the Pripet Marshes.

The data presented is not in fact complete, because on the list there are only aircraft captured on the bigger airfields. Probably no aircraft which force-landed away from airfields are not included.

Table No 1.

Number of combat aircraft produced in the USSR during 1941

Aircraft Type	Months of 1941						Total	Month Jul - Dec	Total in 1941
	Jan	Feb	March	Apr.	May	June			
I-16	-	-	88	-	-	-	88	-	88
I-153	-	-	39	-	1	22	62	-	62
Yak-1	38	9	96	-	134	58	335	776	1111
LaGG-3	-	7	35	-	154	126	322	1596	1918
MiG-3	-	7	474	249	175	384	1289	1569	2858
Su-2	-	-	157	-	136	69	362	443	805
DB-3F	-	-	252	-	87	60	399	315	714
Yer-2	-	-	-	-	17	23	40	67	107
Pe-2	-	-	66	-	219	173	458	1014	1472
SB	-	-	121	-	1	-	122	-	122
Ar-2	-	-	109	-	-	-	109	7	116
Yak2/4	-	-	41	-	22	-	63	36	99
TB-7 (Pe-8)	-	-	2	-	1	6	9	9	18
U-2VS	-	-	-	-	-	-	-	1009	1009
Il-2	-	-	2	-	89	158	249	1061	1310
UTI-4	-	-	254	-	-	-	254	-	254
Total	38	23	1736	249	1036	1079	4161	7902	12063

Table No 2.
Soviet Front and Army Aviation Aircraft in the Five Western Military Districts, June 1941.

Type of Aircraft	Military Districts					Total
	Leningrad	Baltic	Western	Kiev	Odessa	
FIGHTERS						
G. Gladiator	-	2	-	-	-	2
DI-6	-	-	-	15	-	15
I-153	222	364	269	515	143	1513
I-15	6	29	35	16	19	105
I-15bis (I-152)	93	48	64	87	2	294
I-16	395	160	417	455	344	1771
LaGG-3	2	-	-	-	-	2
Miles Hawk	-	1	-	-	-	1
MiG-1	-	31	37	1	8	77
MiG-3	164	109	201	190	181	845
Yak-1	20	3	20	62	-	105
Total	902	747	1043	1341	697	4730
BOMBERS						
SB	349	413	384	276	224	1646
TB-3	1	-	1	-	-	2
Yak-2	-	-	12	73	-	85
Yak-4	-	-	16	20	-	36
Su-2	-	-	89	99	21	209
Total	350	413	502	468	245	1978
DIVE BOMBERS						
Ar-2	23	24	22	23	23	115
Pe-2	21	16	54	74	40	205
Total	44	40	76	97	63	320
GROUND-ATTACK AIRCRAFT						
Il-2	-	5	8	5	-	18
Total	-	5	8	5	-	18
RECONNAISSANCE AIRCRAFT						
R-6	-	1	-	-	-	1
R-ZET	11	-	108	48	10	177
S-2	-	-	9	11	-	20
KOR-1	-	3	-	-	-	3
KOR-2	-	3	-	-	-	3
R-10	-	-	19	25	13	57
R-5	13	12	5	27	13	70
SSS	16	41	1	37	-	95
Anbo IV/41	-	14	-	-	-	14
Anbo 51	-	3	-	-	-	3
Total	40	77	142	148	36	443
TOTAL COMBAT AIRCRAFT						
	1336	1282	1771	2059	1041	7489

Yak-4 light bomber destroyed by German bombs. In the background are some more aircraft of that type and SB bomber.

Table No. 3.

AIRCRAFT USED IN THE FIRST PHASE OF OPERATION BARBAROSSA

Type of aircraft	VVS aircraft in the western part of USSR				*Luftwaffe* and German Army aircraft [1]
	FA and AAv	DBA	VVS-VMF	TOTAL	
Fighters	4730	-	763	5493	793
Zerstörer	-	-	-	-	78
Bombers	1978	1339	337	3654	929
Dive bombers	320	-	-	320	376
Ground-attack	18	-	-	18	60
Reconnaissance		-	352		102
Army recce & liaison aircraft	443	-	-	788	556
Other		-	-		60
Total	7489	1339	1452	10280	2954 [2]

1. According to Ch. Bergström and A. Mikhailov
2. To this should be added about 980 aircraft of the German's allies, and 200 German fighters and Zerstörer aircraft in reserve.

Table No. 4.

VVS IN THE WESTERN USSR *ORDER OF BATTLE, 22 JUNE, 1941*

FRONT AND ARMY AVIATION

LENINGRAD MILITARY DISTRICT
(later Northern Front)

1 SAD (Murmansk)
- · 137 SBAP (Afrikanda) - 38 SB
- · 145 IAP - 56 I-16
- · 147 IAP - 19 I-15bis, 34 I-153

55 SAD (Petrozavodsk)
- · 72 SBAP - 35 SB
- · 265 ShAP - I-15bis, I-153

5 SAD (Karelian Isthmus)
- · ?
- · ?

41 BAD (Siverskaya)
- · 10 SBAP - 40 SB
- · 202 SBAP - 15 SB
- · 205 SBAP - SB
- · 261 SBAP - SB

2 SAD (South of Leningrad)
- · 2 SBAP - 35 SB, Ar-2
- · 44 SBAP - 40 SB
- · 58 SBAP - 30 SB, 16 Pe-2
- · ? IAP - ?

39 IAD (South of Leningrad)
- · 7 IAP - I-16, MiG-3

- · 44 IAP - I-16
- · 148 IAP - I-16
- · 158 IAP - 20 Yak-1
- · 191 IAP - I-16

3 IAD (PVO Leningrad)
- · 19 IAP - ?
- · 26 IAP - ?
- · 153 IAP - MiG-3
- · 157 IAP - ?

54 IAD (PVO Leningrad)
- · 192 IAP - ?
- · 193 IAP - ?
- · 194 IAP - ?
- · 195 IAP - ?

Four KAEs

BALTIC SPECIAL MILITARY DISTRICT
(later Northwestern Front)

4 SAD (Tallin)
- · 63 SBAP - 43 SB
- · ?
- · ?

6 SAD (Riga)
- · 21 IAP - I-16
- · 148 IAP (Libau) - ?
- · 238 IAP - ?

· 239 IAP   - I-16
· 40 SBAP   - 63 SB

7 SAD (Siauliai)
· 10 IAP (Telsiai)   - I-16
· 9 SBAP (Panevezys)   - SB
· 31 SBAP   - SB
· 46 SBAP (Siauliai)   - SB

8 SAD (Kaunas)
· 5 ShAP (Kedainiai)   - I-153
· 13 IAP (Kaunas)   - I-153
· 15 IAP (Alytus)   - I-153
· 31 IAP (Kaunas/Alytus) - 37 MiG-3, I-16

57 SAD (Wilno)
· 54 SBAP (Varena)   - SB
· 42 IAP (Wilno)   - I-15bis (?)
· 49 IAP (Daugavpils)   - I-15bis
· 237 IAP (Wilno ?)   - I-15bis (?)

312 RAP (Kaunas)
nine KAEs, among them:
· 3 KAE (Wilno)
· 10 KAE (Telsiai)
· 11 KAE (Siauliai)
· 16 KAE (Kaunas)
· 29 KAE (Ukmerge)   - 9 ANBO-41,
                           5 ANBO IV,
                           3 ANBO-51,
                           2 Klemm Kl35,
                           1(2) G. Gladiator

WESTERN SPECIAL MILITARY DISTRICT
(Later Western Front)

11 SAD (Lida)
· 16 SBAP (Lesiszcze)   - SB, Pe-2
· 122 IAP (Grodno)   - 75 I-16
· 127 IAP (Lida)   - I-15bis, I-153, I-16

9 SAD (Białystok)
· 13 SBAP (Borysowszczyzna) - 29 SB, 22 Ar-2
· 41 IAP (Białystok)   - 56 MiG-3, 52 I-153
· 124 IAP (Wys. Mazowieckie) - 70 MiG-3
· 126 IAP (Dołubowo)   - 50 MiG-3, 23 I-16
· 129 IAP (Tarnovo)   - 57 MiG-3, 52 I-153

10 SAD (Kobryń)
· 39 SBAP (Pińsk)   - 45 SB, 10 Pe-2
· 74 ShAP (Małyje Zvody) - 70 I-15bis, 8 Il-2

· 33 IAP (Brześć, Prużany)- I-15bis, I-153, I-16
· 123 IAP (Kobryń)   - I-16, 20 Yak-1

43 IAD (Orsha)
· 160 IAP (Minsk)   - 60 I-153
· 161 IAP (Minsk)   - 62 I-16
· 162 IAP (Mogilev)   - 54 I-16
· 163 IAP (Mogilev)   - 59 I-16

12 BAD (Vitebsk)
· 6 SBAP (Demidov)   - SB
· 12 SBAP   - SB
· 43 BBAP (Demidov)   - 20 Su-2, 30 R-ZET
· 161 RAP (Karachi)   - SB, R-5

13 BAD (Bobruysk)
· 24 SBAP (Bobruysk)   - SB
· 27 SBAP (Bobruysk)   - SB
· 121 SBAP (Rogachev)   - SB
· 125 SBAP (Rogachev)   - SB
· 130 SBAP (Bobrowicze) - SB
· 97 BBAP (Bobruysk)   - 50 Su-2

eight KAEs

KIEV SPECIAL MILITARY DISTRICT
(Later Southwestern Front)

14 SAD (Łuck)
· 17 IAP (Kovel)   - I-16, Yak-1
· 46 IAP (Dubno)   - I-16, Yak-1
· 89 IAP   - I-16, Yak-1
· 253 ShAP   - I-15bis
· 315 RAP   - ?

15 SAD (Lwów)
· 23 IAP   - I-16, MiG-3
· 28 IAP (Lwów)   - 7 I-16, 36 MiG-3
· 164 IAP (Kurovice)   - I-16, MiG-3
· 66 ShAP (Kurovice)   - I-153
· 37 RAP   - SB

16 SAD (Tarnopol)
· 87 IAP (Tarnopol)   - 60 I-16, 4 MiG-3
· 92 IAP   - I-16, I-153
· 86 SBAP (Trembowla)   - SB
· 88 SBAP   - SB

63 SAD (Stryj)
· 64 ShAP   - 64 I-153
· 165 IAP   - I-16, I-153

64 SAD (Stanisławów)

· ? SBAP	- SB, Ar-2
· 12 IAP (Stanisławów)	- 66 I-153
· 149 IAP	- I-16, 21 MiG-3
· 166 IAP	- I-16
· 247 IAP	- ?

17 SAD (Proskurov)

· 20 IAP	- 60 I-153, Yak-1
· 91 IAP	- 66 I-153, 4 I-15bis, - 4 Yak-1
· 48 SBAP	- SB
· 225 SBAP	- SB

62 BAD (Kiev)

· 52 SBAP	- SB, Pe-2
· 94 SBAP	- SB, Pe-2
· 226 BBAP (Zulyamy)	- Su-2
· 227 BBAP (Borodyanka)	- Su-2
· 243 ShAP	- I-15bis, I-153, 5 Il-2
· 245 ShAP	- ?

19 BAD (Biala Tserkov)

· 14 SBAP	- SB, Ar-2, Pe-2
· 33 SBAP	- SB, Ar-2
· 136 BBAP	- 49 Yak-2, 5 Yak-4
· 138 SBAP	- SB, Su-2

44 IAD (Vinnitsa)

· 3 IAP	- I-16
· ?	
· ?	

Eleven KAEs

ODESSA MILITARY DISTRICT
(later Southern Front)

20 SAD

· 4 IAP (Revaka)	- I-16, I-153, MiG-3
· 55 IAP (Beltsy)	- I-16, I-153, MiG-3
· 45 SBAP	- SB
· 211 BBAP (Kotovsk)	- Su-2

21 SAD (Odessa)

· 5 SBAP	- 30 SB, 20 Pe-2
· 67 IAP (Bolgrad)	- I-16
· 69 IAP (Odessa)	- 70 I-16, 5 MiG-3
· 299 ShAP	- I-15bis

45 SAD

· 132 SBAP (Kirovograd)	- SB, Ar-2
· 168 IAP	- I-16

· 210 BBAP (Kirovograd)	- Su-2
· 246 IAP	- I-16
· 160 RAP	- ?
317 RAP	- SB
Four KAEs	

LONG-RANGE BOMBER AVIATION

1 BOMBER AVIATION CORPS
(Novgorod)

40 AD (Krechvitsy)	- 1DB-3F
· 53 DBAP (Krechvitsy)	- 55 DB-3
· 200 DBAP (Krechvitsy)	- 38 DB-3F
· 7 TBAP (Soltsy)	- 68 TB-3
51 AD (Yedrovo)	- 1DB-3F
· 7 DBAP (Yedrovo)	- 30 DB-3/DB-3F
· 203 DBAP (Yedrovo)	- 48 DB-3/DB-3F
· 204 DBAP (Yedrovo)	- 33 DB-3

---

2 BOMBER AVIATION CORPS
(Kursk)

35 AD (Bryansk)	- 2 DB-3F
· 100 DBAP (Orel)	- 71 DB-3/DB-3F
· 219 DBAP (Bryansk)	- 46 DB-3F
· 223 DBAP (Karachev)	- 6 (?) DB-3F
48 AD (Kursk)	- 4 DB-3, TB-3
· 51 DBAP (Kursk)	- 58 DB-3
· 220 DBAP (Kursk)	- 15 DB-3
· 221 DBAP (Shchigry)	- 35 DB-3
· 222 DBAP (Oboyan)	- 14 DB-3

---

3 BOMBER AVIATION CORPS
(Smolensk)

52 AD (Shatalovo)	- 1 DB-3F
· 3 TBAP (Sesha)	- 52 TB-3
· 98 DBAP (Shatalovo)	- 70 DB-3F
· 212 DBAP (Smolensk)	- 61 DB-3F
42 AD (Borovskoe)	- 3 DB-3F
· 1 TBAP (Shaykovka)	- 41 TB-3
· 96 DBAP (Borovskoe)	- 50 DB-3F
· 207 DBAP (Borovskoe)	- 16 DB-3F

4 BOMBER AVIATION CORPS
(Zaporozhe)

22 AD (Zaporozhe)   - 1 DB-3F
 · 8 DBAP (Zaporozhe)   - 69 DB-3F
 · 11 DBAP (Zaporozhe)   - 54 DB-3/DB-3F
 · 21 DBAP (Saki)   - 72 DB-3/DB-3F
50 AD (Rostov-on-Don)   - 3 DB-3F
 · 81 DBAP (Novocherkassk)- 61 DB-3F
 · 228 DBAP (Novocherkassk)- 10 DB-3/DB-3F
 · 231 DBAP (Rostov)   - 19 DB-3
 · 299 DBAP (Rostov)   - 56 DB-3F

18 LONG-RANGE BOMBER AVIATION DIVISION
(INDEPENDENT)

Command of the division (Skomorokhy) - 3 DB-3F
 · 14 TBAP (Borispol)   - 38 TB-3, 9 TB-7
 · 90 DBAP (Skomorokhy) - 60 DB-3F
 · 93 DBAP (Skomorokhy) - 58 DB-3F

SOVIET NAVAL AVIATION

NORTHERN FLEET

72 SAP   - 4 I-16, 28 I-15bis,
                     17 I-153, 11 SB
118 OMRAP   - 37 MBR-2,
                     7 GST (PBY/Catalina)
49 ORAE   -17 MBR-2

Total – 121 aircraft

BALTIC FLEET

8 BAB
 · 1 MTAP   - DB-3. DB-3T, SB
 · 57 BAP   - SB
61 IAB
 · 5 IAP   - I-16, I-153
 · 13 IAP   - I-16, I-153
10 SAB
 · 73 BAP   - SB, R-10
 · 71 IAP   - I-153, 8 Yak-1
 · 15 OMRAP   - 40 MBR-2
seven independent fighter squadrons: 15; 41;
     43; 44; 58; 71; 81 – I-16, I-153

Total – 707 aircraft

BLACK SEA FLEET

62 IAB
 · 8 IAP   - I-16, I-15bis, I-153
 · 32 IAP   - I-16
63 BAB
 · 2 MTAP   - DB-3, DB-3F, DB-3T
 · 40 BAP   - SB
 · 62 BAP   - SB
116 OMRAP   - MBR-2, GST,
                       2 MTB-2
119 OMRAP   - MBR-2, GST
eleven independent fighter and maritime reconnaissance squadrons – I-16, I-153, MBR-2

Total – 624 aircraft

The airfield at Minsk was captured by the Germans on 29 June 1941. On the right: wrecks of I-153. On the left: U-2, USB, another U-2 and a tail of PS-84 (DC-3) with yellow tactical number "6" on its rudder.

Table no 5.

Aircraft type	Captured by *Luftflotte* No.:	Aircraft in condition (*Zustand*):			Aircraft Total
		I/II	III	IV	
FIGHTERS					
Polikarpov I-16	1	38	51	30	119
	2	7	6	6	19
	4	-	9	-	9
Polikarpov I-153	1	-	-	4	4
	2	-	-	5	5
	4	1	13	7	21
Polikarpov I-15	1	11	41	11	63
	2	3	21	25	49
	4	-	37	3	40
MiG-3 [1]	1	27	20	24	71
	4	-	7	1	8
Gloster Gladiator [2]	1	11	2	-	13
Dewoitine D-501 [3]	1	12	-		12
Fiat CR 20 [4]	1	3	4	-	7
Fighters Total	-	113	211	116	440
BOMBERS and DIVE-BOMBERS					
SB-2M-100 [5]	1	8	18	14	40
	2	7	9	7	23
SB-2M-103 [6]	1	5	30	16	51
	2	4	7	6	17
	4	-	2	3	5
DB-3	1	-	12	2	14
	2	-	1	-	1
	4	-	1	3	4
DB-3F [7]	1	-	1	1	2
	2	1	1	-	2
TB-3	1	-	3	3	6
Su-2 [8]	2	5	-	-	5
Pe-2	1	-	2	-	2
	2	6	3	2	11
	4	1	1	-	2
Bombers Total	-	37	91	57	185
RECONNAISSANCE AIRCRAFT					
R-5	1	14	7	-	21
	2	-	2	-	2
	4	-	4	2	6
R-ZET	1	-	8	5	13
	2	1	2	-	3
	4	-	2	-	2
Tupolev R-6	1	1	1	-	2
R-10	4	-	5	-	5
Anbo 41 [9]	1	-	10	7	17
Anbo 51 [10]	1	-	3	-	3
Total		16	44	14	74
TRAINING AIRCRAFT and OTHERS					
UTI-4 [11]	1	3	6	1	10
	2	3	16	-	19
	4	-	12		12
UT-1	1	7	3	-	10
	2	3	-	-	3
UT-2	1	6	11	2	19
	2	4	2	-	6

Aircraft					Total
U-2	1	5	-	3	8
	4	-	2	4	6
Udet A-12A Flamingo [12]	1	-	2	-	2
LVG C-VI [13]	1	-	-	2	2
Taylorcraft Cub J2 [14]	2	1	-	-	1
Piper Cub J3 [15]	2	1	-	-	1
Percival Q6 [16]	1	1	-	-	1
DH-89 Dragon Rapide [17]	1	-	1	-	1
	2	2	-	-	2
DH-60 "Moth" [18]	1	-	1	-	1
Cierva C.30 [19]	2	1	1	-	2
Farman F-393 [20]	2	1	-	-	1
Caudron C.280 [21]	2	1	-	-	1
VEF I-12 [22]	1	2	-	-	2
PWS-16/26 [23]	1	33	-	1	34
RWD-8 [24]	1	25	3	-	28
"Wrona" Glider [25]	2	11	-	-	11
"Czajka" Glider [26]	4	-	30	3	33
Blind-flying tool	1	-	1	-	1
Total		111	90	16	217
AIRCRAFT MISIDENTIFIED AND OF UNKNOWN TYPE					
ZKB-19 Fighter [27]	1	5	2	-	7
	2	40	9	-	49
	4	-	13	-	13
S-16 Fighter [28]	1	1	9	7	17
I-17 Fighter [29]	1	-	-	1	1
	4	1	2	1	4
Finnish fighter [30]	4	-	9	-	9
I-100B Fighter [31]	4	-	1	-	1
I-200A Fighter [32]	4	-	-	1	1
Obsolete fighter, unknown type	4	-	2	-	2
Bomber unknown type	1	-	1	-	1
	2	2	1	-	3
	4	5	-	3	8
F-153 bomber [33]	2	-	17	-	17
IA-2 destroyer [34]	2	1	3	-	4
Destroyer unknown type [35]	4	-	2	-	2
Recce, high-wing, a/c [36]	1	1	-	-	1
Czech biplane [37]	1	-	4	-	4
Sailplanes [38]	1	1	-	-	1
	2	18	3	-	21
Polish a/c RWD type 46 [39]	1	7	3	-	10
Polish a/c type 46 [40]	1	2	-	-	2
Unknown Rata trainers [41]	1	2	2	-	4
	2	-	2	-	2
Biplane trainers	1	-	3	-	3
High-wing trainers [42]	1	-	-	5	5
Unknown type trainers	1	4	2	30	36
	2	-	11	25	36
	4	6	9	1	16
A-c unknown	4	1	-	-	1
Sport a-c unknown	1	-	-	1	1
	2	1	5	-	6
	4	-	5	12	17
Passenger a-c unknown	1	-	-	1	1
Scrap unknown	1	-	-	115	115
	2	-	-	12	12
	4	-	-	7	7
Total		98	120	223	441
Total all aircraft		375	556	426	1357

Note:
Zustand I – means that aircraft was in factory condition or new.
Zustand II – in operational condition
Zustand III – aircraft usable but required repair
Zustand IV – aircraft to scrap

Remarks:
1. In the original documents, I-61 and I-18. There was no MiG-3 name in German documents, however the author has an original German photos of MiG-3 with German caption I-61 or I-18. Aircraft captured by Luftflotte 1 included 20-16-12 of the "I-61" and 7-4-12 "I-18". All MiGs-3 captured by Luftflotte 4 were called "I-18".
2. Lithuanian and Latvian aircraft captured by the Soviets in 1940, and in 1941 by the Germans at Siauliai and Krustpils
3. Lithuanian aircraft captured at Palanga
4. Former Lithuanian aircraft
5. In original "SB-2"
6. In original "SB-3" – "combat aircraft" that means not USB version
7. In original DB-3a
8. In original "Zerstörer S.U."
9. Lithuanian aircraft
10. As above. In original "Anbo 15"
11. In original "Jagdumschlflzg. Rata I/16"
12. Latvian aircraft
13. German WWI reconnaissance type. Used by Lithuanian Aviation till 1940.
14,15. Original document included 2 Taylorcraft Cubs. It is known that only one of them, belonging to the Lithuanian "Riflemen's Union", was a Taylorcraft, but the second was a Piper Cub which belonged in 1940 to Lietuvos Aeroklubas
16. One of two passenger aircraft used by Lithuanian Airlines (Lietuvos Oro Linijos)

17. Originally "De Haviland Dragonfly". This aircraft was not used in Russia or the Baltic Countries. It is known that Germans captured Latvian and Lithuanian DH-98 Dragon Rapides.
18. Ex-Lithuanian aircraft
19. As above. Captured at Aukstagiris
20. As above
21. As above
22. In original "Jagdschuflzg VEF I-12". In fact it was not a fighter-trainer, but a sports aircraft belonging to Latvian Aviation
23. Polish training aircraft, which on 18.09.1939, flew to Latvia, the day after the Soviet invasion.
24. As above
25. Polish gliders captured by the Lithuanians in 1939 and later by the Germans at Aukstagiris.
26. Polish gliders captured by the Germans at Lwów
27. ZKB 19 – almost certainly I-153.
28. Probably Polikarpov I-16. Some publications stated that it could be Letov S-16.
29. Unknown type – probably Yak-1
30. Unknown.
31. Unknown
32. Probably MiG-1
33. Probably I-153 with bomb racks. There are many photos of captured I-153s, but in the table under "Fighters" the Germans listed only 30 I-153.
34. Probably Yak-2/4
35. As above
36. Probably ex-Lithuanian Ansaldo A120 or Anbo IV
37. Probably Letov S-16
38. Probably Russian MBR-2
39. Aircraft evacuated to Baltic countries in 1939, probably RWD-8 or even RWD-14 Czapla
40. As above. It could be PWS-16/PWS-26.
41. Probably UTI-2 or UT-1.
42. Probably an Anbo type.

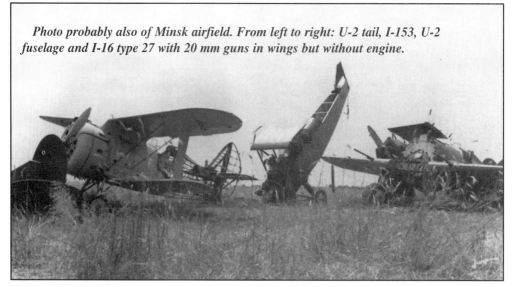

Photo probably also of Minsk airfield. From left to right: U-2 tail, I-153, U-2 fuselage and I-16 type 27 with 20 mm guns in wings but without engine.

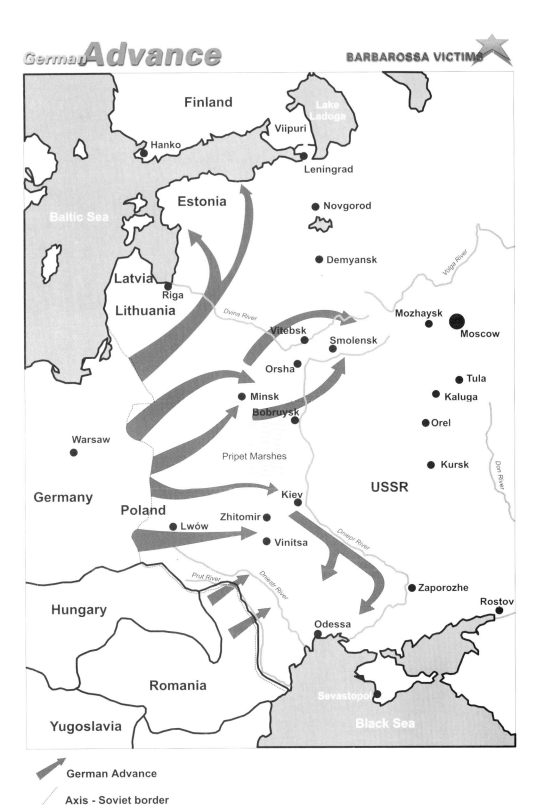

German Advance

Axis - Soviet border

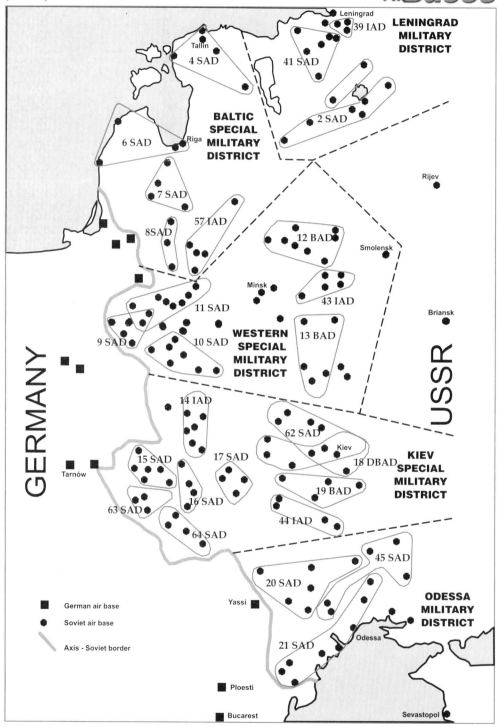

Leningrad

39 IAD

**LENINGRAD
MILITARY
DISTRICT**

41 SAD

Tallin

4 SAD

2 SAD

**BALTIC
SPECIAL
MILITARY
DISTRICT**

Rijev

6 SAD

Riga

7 SAD

57 IAD

8SAD

Smolensk

12 BAD

Minsk

43 IAD

11 SAD

Briansk

WESTERN
SPECIAL
MILITARY
DISTRICT

13 BAD

9 SAD

10 SAD

USSR

GERMANY

14 IAD

62 SAD

Kiev

18 DBAD

**KIEV
SPECIAL
MILITARY
DISTRICT**

15 SAD

17 SAD

Tarnów

19 BAD

16 SAD

63 SAD

44 IAD

64 SAD

45 SAD

20 SAD

Yassi

**ODESSA
MILITARY
DISTRICT**

21 SAD

Odessa

■ German air base

● Soviet air base

／ Axis - Soviet border

Ploesti

Bucarest

Sevastopol

Left:

Group of five ex-Latvian Gloster **Gladiator Mk I's**, which were captured at Krustpils airfield in summer of 1941. Aircraft in the foreground carries the badge of one of the Latvian Squadrons equipped with Gladiators, and the black number "168" (?). All Latvian Gladiators were bought from the UK in 1937, and carried numbers from 114 to 126 and from 163 to 175.

Above:

Different group of ex-Latvian **Gladiators**, used by the Russians. Note that one of them still wears the badge of its Latvian Squadron and Latvian number. A Russian star was painted over the Latvian swastika after 17 June 1940, when Russia invaded the Baltic countries and took over all their armament. A year later, during the German attack, some of the Latvian and Lithuanian aircraft were destroyed. Still eleven Gladiators (mostly Latvian), and in very good condition and two damaged aircraft were intercepted by the Germans. Some of them were used as glider tugs (for DFS 230) in training unit Erg. Gr. (S) 1 at Langendiebach near Hanau.

Left:

Ex-Lithuanian **Gladiator Mk I** no. G-709 captured at Siauliai Base in Lithuania, June 1941. This Gladiator was among fourteen machines bought from the UK in 1938. After annexation of Lithuania by the Soviet Union in 1940, Lithuanian national markings on wings and rudder were painted over. Most of the Lithuanian Gladiators were destroyed during German air attacks, so only a few survived to be later used by Erg. Gr. (S)1.

Above:

Polikarpov I-5 captured by the Germans, displaying white "6" on the tail. In the early thirties the Russians built 803 of I-5 fighters. In early 1939 89 of them were used in combat units, and some of them were still in use during the German attack in 1941. Equipped with two bomb racks under the fuselage (see photo), they were used as ground attack aircraft. On 1 October 1941 11 ShAP still had 20 I-5s, and these aircraft were used close to Sevastopol.

Right:

Wreck of an **I-5** photographed somewhere in Southern Russia. Rear part of the fuselage unveils unusual three-colour camouflage is still visible, and partial red star. Brand new I-5 fighters could reach a maximum speed of 252 km/h at 5,000m and 278 km/h close to the ground. In 1941 the I-5 was totally obsolete.

Left:

I-15bis (**I-152**) abandoned by the Russians at one of hundreds of airfields. I-15bis was almost as vintage as the **I-5** type, but during German attack **I-15bis** were still used in 10 fighter squadrons (268 aircraft, including 27 unserviceable). 145 **I-15bis** were used by Naval Aviation (29 in Red Banner Baltic Sea Naval Aviation).

Left:

Wreck of **I-15bis,** white "11". German soldier is examining this interesting aircraft.

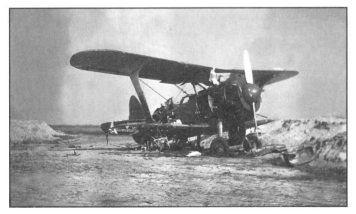

Left:

Similar aircraft but still with its spinner. **I-15bis** were equipped with bomb racks for four 25 kg or 32 kg bombs and were usually used as ground attack aircraft.

Right:

The same aircraft, but showing more damage. Note that wing struts were painted in the underside colour on the top half, and uppersurface colour on the lower half.

Right:

Burned-out wreck of an **I-15bis** at the airfield in Kovno (Kaunas). In the background is a **Bf109F** of II Gruppe of one of the German Geschwaders.

Right:

German soldier examining the cockpit of an **I-15bis**.

Above:
Undersurface of a shot down **I-15bis**.

Below:
Airfield at Wilno after it was captured by the Germans. There is an **SB** bomber in the background, **I-153** in the centre and **I-15bis** to the right. The latter has wheel covers, but no red stars, which were cut off. Russians stars were among the most prized war trophies with German troops.

I-153, number "3" stripped down by its conquerors. Photo taken at the airfield at Borisov. This aircraft is rather unusual because it has a radio installed (air mast on the right upper wing). It also has RS-82 rocket rails (four of them under each wing). Rockets were used mostly during ground attack missions.

Left:

Souvenir from Russia. Once again the **I-153** fighter with radio equipment installed, and tactical number "3". No rocket rails but with bomb racks.

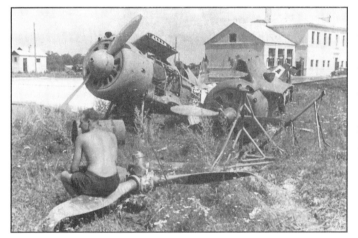

Left:

Pair of light gray or silver **I-153** wrecks at one of the Soviet air bases. Aircraft to the left with older **I-15bis** style spinner. **I-153** to the right has new version of the spinner.

Left:

I-153 in overall aluminium or light grey dope, showing evidence of repairs to the fabric covering. Yellow "7" with black trim and illegible serial number in front of "7". **I-15bis** and **Hs 126** visible in the background.

Right:

I-153 painted in the same way. Port lower wing is very heavily patched, and appears to be still in primer. Note pre-war style red star, with black circle in the centre.

Right:

I-153 captured in Lwów with bomb racks under its wings. The fabric covering of the rear portion of fuselage and tail has been stripped off, showing the underlying framework.

Right:

I-153 with damaged skin of the port wings. Number "10" on the rudder probably in red.

Left:

Silver or light grey **I-153** number "6" with four bomb racks at Alytus airfield. Aircraft belonged to 42 IAP, and at the time of the photo was still in very good condition.

Left, below:

Group of **I-153**s with completely different camouflage pattern, showing the transition in operational VVS colours at this time. To the right is an **I-153** in light grey, in the centre one in dark green/ light blue, and behind to the left is a silver or grey aircraft with a sloppily applied and patchy dark colour (green?).

Below:

Similar group of captured **I-153**s, at Wilno airfield this time, 2 July 1941. To the right and to the left are aircraft in dark green camouflage and two silver/light grey I-153s with rather patchy finish in the centre. All **I-153**s have tactical numbers ("2", "3", "13" and "12"). **R-5** and **U-2** are also visible.

Above and right:

Silver **I-153** captured somewhere in Lithuania. Aircraft with red (or blue) top to the rudder. Both photos show very well how I-153s were painted.

Below:

Silver **I-153,** "52", suggesting that numbers in Soviet units were continuous.

Above:

I-153 with illegible tactical number on the rudder. I-153 was the last of the Polikarpov biplane fighters in mass production. Armed with 4 machine guns, and the maximum speed just above 400 km/h.

Left:

This wreck of I-153 shows details of the construction, wing ribs, fuel tank and fuselage framework.

Right:

Similar shot once again shows fuselage details and undersurfaces, i.e. wheel wells and bomb racks. Bomb racks were installed to improve the ground attack capabilities of the **I-153**.

Below:

Collection of **I-15bis** and **I-153** frameworks. Note the tail constructions details.

Left:

Where bomb racks were not fitted, **I-153**s usually had RS-82 rocket rails, as seen here.

Left and below:

I-153 number "15", not ready for combat, was abandoned at its airfield. On the right upper wing the aerial mast could be easily seen. Radios were mounted only in the commanders' aircraft.

Right:

Another shot of an **I-153** with RS-82 rocket rails, this time number "1". The pilot damaged the fuselage, but German souvenir hunters cut out the red stars off of the wings.

Below:

Silver or light grey **I-153** number "11", probably from no.1 squadron of the regiment.

Right:

I-153s removed from combat duty and stored on the airfield. Both aircraft with bomb racks, and one in the background also showing RS-82 rails. Photo was taken at Kiejdany, Lithuania.

Left:

One more **I-153** hidden in the forest. Probably an old tactical number was painted over and the new one, "3", added.

Left:

I-153, damaged in combat, on its nose after landing, end of June 1941. Markings typical for pre-war VVS, red stars on the fuselage and on the wings with black trim and black circle.

Left:

The same aircraft photographed a little bit later. Note the tactical number and a hole through the vertical stabiliser. Wreck of **MiG-3**, and **Fi-156** Storch (SI+P?) and **Ju-52,** in the background.

Right:

I-153, probably light grey, number "29". In Soviet regiments the tactical numbers were continuous (from 1 to 65), sometimes with different colours for different squadrons. This photo was probably taken at Minsk, so this **I-153** was of 160 IAP, because only that regiment of 42 IAD was equipped with the I-153 fighters.

Right:

In the background the same **I-153,** "29" and the wreck of a different aircraft with a German soldier in the foreground.

Right:

I-153 photographed at the same airfield with very interesting camouflage. Small dark green patches were applied (probably by brush) over the silver (or gray) background. An order to camouflage all aircraft in that way was issued in the middle of June 1941 but only a few aircraft were so repainted. Red or yellow number "63", with black trim, on the rudder.

Left:

On the right the same **I-153** with number "63". Note that upper wing tip is without patches. In the background is a dark green **I-16** number "3" with stars on its wings.

Left, below:

Once more the same **I-153** "63" shows the camouflage on the engine cowl. Bomb racks are also visible. Note rudder of the **I-16,** white number "3".

Below:

Former Polish air base at Porubanek close to Wilno, called by Germans Wilno-South, just after capture by German troops. In the foreground is a silver **I-153** with number "10" but with its stars removed. Behind, **I-16** type 5, and **Me110** of ZG 26.

Right:

I-153, with artillery piece in the foreground.

Right:

I-153, not quite ready for action, captured at Orsha airfield.

Right:

Many of these I-153s were probably in flying condition when German souvenir hunters found them.

Right:

Light grey I-153 captured by the Germans, with bomb racks under the wings.

Air base with many wrecked VVS aircraft. The **I-16** to the right is the trainer version -**UTI-4**. About 3,180 of these were built. In the centre **I-16** type 6 and **I-15bis**.

Left:

UTI-4 captured by Germans in very good condition. It is an early version of the UTI-4 with fixed undercarriage and old type canopy. Some early UTI-4s received a one-piece canopy which later became standard.

Left:

Germans captured this late model **UTI-4**, with new version of the canopy and retractable undercarriage, at Varena airfield. The aircraft still in very good condition except it has lost the starboard navigation light. Production of the UTI-4 continued from 1938 to early 1942.

Right:

Pilot of this **UTI-4** was forced to land on a farm-house at Demidov. As a result the aircraft and house were destroyed. A white stripe painted on the left wing denotes probably that this aircraft is not to be used for aerobatics. A German soldier took this photo in September 1941.

Right:

As shown here, laundry was not a problem. Note details of the **UTI-4** and the canopy style. Also a stenciled "brat' zdjes' " (*lift here*) is visible under the tailplane. Visible on the left elevator is the serial number - probably 1815423.

Right:

UTI-4 abandoned by the Russians at Alytus, Lithuania. Note the nose part is in a different colour. Aircraft with retractable undercarriage but with older style of instructor's canopy.

Left:

A pair of **UTI-4**s captured by the Germans in early August 1941. Note that the apparently different colours of wings are due to a different lighting conditions, and not a different paint shade.

Left:

The same **UTI-4** as in the bottom of the previous page but 3/4 front view. Note that red stars under the wings are very close to the fuselage.

Right:

Almost a commercial shot of an **I-16** type 5, at one of the air bases used by the Germans. This version of the I-16 had a "full" canopy, which opened by sliding forward on special rails. Armament was only two ShKAS machine guns.

Right:

I-16s stored in a hangar at one of the air bases around Siauliai, Lithuania. All aircraft in perfect condition, but the Germans never tried to use them.

Right:

Wrecks of **I-16**s showing construction details.

Above:

Line-up of **I-16** type 5s somewhere in Russia. Aircraft with two colour tactical numbers on the rudder, probably red or blue with white trim. German souvenir hunters may have already removed the OP-1 gun sights from the cockpits. First aircraft ("3") has a trestle under the rear part of the fuselage, perhaps for tailwheel repairs - note the fuselage tailcone lying just in front of the trestle.

Above and below:

Two shots of part of the air base where **I-16**, **I-153** and **I-15bis** aircraft were overhauled, July 1941. On the right part of the upper photo and in the lower photo the same **I-16** type 5 no. "1" can be seen.

Right:

I-16 type 6 with modified canopy and PAK-1 gun sight. This version, similar to type 5, had 2 machine guns in the wings. On the rudder tactical no. "15" with white shadow.

Right:

Wreck of **I-16** with very high tactical no. "72". Note the engine mount and wing details.

Right:

I-16 shot down by the Germans, with unit markings on the rudder in the form of a two-colour trim. The tactical no. "60" was also painted in two colours.

Left:

The same **I-16** watched by German troops. It is type 10, the the first I-16 with four machine guns (two in wings and two in fuselage).

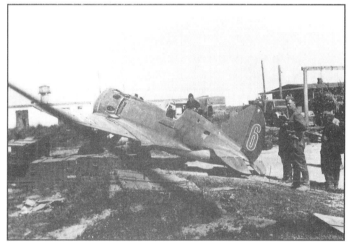

Left:

I-16, probably type 10, abandoned at one of the Russian air bases. On the rudder is a yellow or blue tactical no. "6" with white trim.

Left:

Inspection of **I-16** type 5 abandoned by the Russians during transportation to the airfield, July 1941.

I-16 type 5 abandoned at one of the airfields.

Right:

"Before take off" - German soldier familirizing himself with **I-16** type 5 cockpit.

Right:

One more captured **I-16** type 5. The aircraft still has its OP-1 gun sight. Germans very often removed these gun sights from captured aircraft, to prevent unauthorised use in combat.

Left:

Completely destroyed **I-16** tireless and with stripped down paint on the wooden part of the fuselage. Metal and fabric parts are still painted dark green.

Above and left:

I-16 type 6, silver or grey overall with black trim around the exhaust outlets. Tactical no. "1" as usual on the rudder.

Right:

Intact **I-16** type 5 abandoned at Varena.

Right:

Another **I-16** type 5 abandoned by the Russians, this time slightly damaged. Tactical no. "7" very unusual - in black.

Right:

Scrapyard at one of the Soviet air bases, probably Minsk. In the foreground **I-16** type 27 with ShVAK 20 mm guns in the wings and two ShKAS machine guns over the engine. Aircraft probably from one of the 43 IAD regiments - 161, 162 or 163 IAP. All their I-16s probably carried the white lightning flash across the fin and rudder (as seen on white "6" and yellow "11")

Left:

The same place but photo taken from a different direction. **I-16** with patched and repainted areas of the wing. Second **I-16** with tactical no. "8".

Left:

Once more, the same group of **I-16s**. All aircraft show the lightning flash motif - probably a regimental marking.

Left:

I-16 type 5 with no. "1" and coloured fin tip. Photo taken at Siauliai, Lithuania. Note wing details, and the aircraft in the background - SB with no. "12", Lithuanian Gladiator and two Ansaldo A-120s, one without engine.

Right:

Two photos of **I-16** type 5 tactical no. "8" captured by the Germans, probably at Mitau airfield, Latvia. Note the canopy rails and coloured fin tip. Colour of the fin tip is not certain, but could be blue or yellow.

Below:

Line-up of different **I-16**s of the same unit. In the first row **I-16** type 5, with **I-16** type 10 behind. Also **UTI-4** and **U-2, SB** and **I-153**.

Left and below:

Two shots of **I-16** type 5 with tactical no. "2" and SL-17 camera gun behind the cockpit. On later types the PAU-22 camera gun was mounted instead. Siauliai airfield, summer 1941.

Left:

Photo of **I-16** type 5 of the same regiment but with darker tactical no. "9".

Left:

The same **I-16** no. "9", viewed from the rear. In the background, R-5 and SB of 46 SBAP.

Siauliai airfield, June 1941. On the right three **I-16** type 5 of two or three different squadrons of one regiment. On the left, **MiG-3** and **SB**. An **Ar-2** is also visible.

Right:

Close up of **I-16** type 10 with unusual camouflage. Most of the I-16s were in two-tone (green/blue) camouflage, but this one is silver or light grey with brushed irregular green patches. In the background other I-16s with lightning flashes on the fin/rudder. The photo was taken probably at Minsk.

Right:

I-16 type 5 with white tactical no. "6" on the rudder.

Left:
  Another souvenir photo, this time with **I-16** type 6. Serial number painted on the tail (*621528 or 821528*) suggest this aircraft had just had been through a general overhaul.

Left:
  German soldier looking for the red star under the wing. The most wanted souvenir from Russia.

Left:
  Two German soldiers with **I-16** type 16 or type 24 with stars cut away. Both versions of I-16 had armament identical to the **I-16** type 10 (four mg-s), but different engines. Type 16 had Shvetsov M-62 1000 HP engine, while type 24 used M-63 1100 HP engine.

Right and below:

I-16 type 6 after forced landing. This aircraft has no tactical numbers.

Right:

Pilot of this **I-16** type 6 also made a forced landing. Hole in the fuselage is probably where a red star used to be.

Left and below:

I-16 type 29 with yellow number "4", but no star on the fuselage! Type 29 was the last version of the I-16, armed with 2 ShKAS machine guns and 1 12.7 mm Berezin UBS under the engine. With this installation air intake had to be moved around the cowling. Note heavy exhaust stains on the wheel covers.

Right:

Another captured **I-16** type 29, tactical no. "15" this time. UBS machine gun under the engine is visible, and the air intake is to the starboard. This aircraft also has a radio installed, with the aerial fitted to the right side of the engine cowl.

Right:

I-16 type 29 with additional armament. Bomb rack and three RS-82 rocket rails under each wing.

Right and next page:

Slightly damaged **I-16** type 29 with no. "9", abandoned by the Russians on the forest border. The aircraft has RS-82 rocket rails and RSI-3 radio installation with aerial visible above the cockpit.

Below:
German airmen at the captured airfield. On the left **I-16** type 29 no. "6", in the middle a damaged Hs 126, and a **MiG-3** to the right.

MiG-1 captured by the Germans. Almost identical with its successor the **MiG-3**, the only visible differences beeing the shape of the wheel well covers and a shorter radiator behind the cowling. In the background, **Ar-2** and **Ju 88**.

Right:

Very interesting early **MiG-1** found at one of the Russian air bases. Fuselage without engine, with a canopy similar to the one used on the I-200 prototype. **MiG-1's** were quite rare because only 100 were ever built.

Right:

First **MiG-1**s were sent to combat units in early 1941. Among first to receive them were 41 IAP based at the former Polish airfield at Białystok and 31 IAP based at Kaunas (Kovno) airfield. This photo shows the aircraft belonging to 31 IAP (no. "5" on the fin). In the background are **MiG-3** and **R-5**.

Left:

Two shots of the same group of MiGs. On the left, front part of **MiG-1** (no. "5") with damaged aileron. Note bare metal prop blades and wheel well covers typical for this type of aircraft.

Below:

MiG-3 with different wheel well covers. From January 1941 the **MiG-3** replaced the **MiG-1** on the production lines. Germans captured this fighter at 8 SAD airfield at Alytus, Lithuania.

Right:

MiG-3 (white "2"), captured in intact. Aircraft has radio outfit, installed only on commanders' aircraft. **MiG-3** as compared to **MiG-1**, had engine moved about 10 cm forward, enlarged fuel tanks and longer radiator under the fuselage. Wheels and well covers were also different. In spite of all these changes the aircraft still was very difficult to fly having very low manoeuvrability.

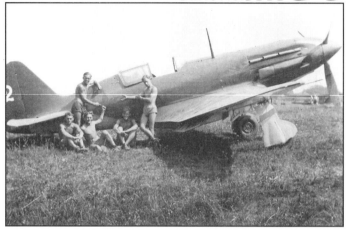

Right:

MiG-3 captured in Lithuania with crudely applied tactical no. "1", probably in yellow.

Right:

Same aircraft, but seen from the opposite side. Note the light repair patch on the rudder, (also visible in the previous photo).

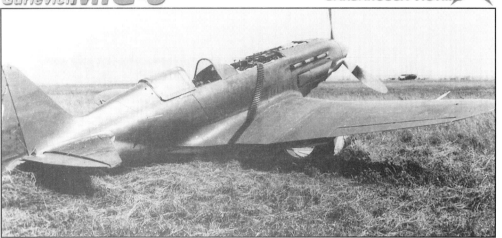

Above and left:

Abandoned **MiG-3** with exposed ammunition belt for UBS 12.7 mm gun. Tactical number "7"

Left:

Same aircraft, but seen from opposite side. Note the damaged wings and repair patches to the rudder.

Right and below:

MiG-3 captured at Kaunas with coloured fin tip and tactical no. "3" on the rudder.

Right:

Mig-3 with radio outfit and tactical no. "8". Note fuselage details. This beautiful plane was very difficult to fly with a high tendency to spin. Heavy losses were often attributed to frequent engine and undercarriage failures during landing and take offs.

Right:

MiGs photographed at air base in Kaunas (Kovno) or Siauliai.

Left:

MiG-3 captured at Siauliai. MiG was designed as a high altitude fighter and it performed best above 6,000m altitude. At low altitudes, where most of the battles were fought, the fighter was heavy and easily outmaneuvered. German pilots noted MiG-3's tendency to spin during low altitude dog-fights

Left:

German soldier examining **MiG-3**'s armament. The aircraft was captured at Kaunas (Kovno). **MiG-3** standard armament consisted of two ShKAS 7.62 mm machine guns and one 12.7 UBS gun. This however was not sufficient firepower against German aircraft. Also, gun synchronisation of poor quality often contributed to serious propellerdamage.

Below:

To increase firepower some early **MiG-3**'s were equipped with additional underwing gun pods housing a UBK 12.7 machine gun. The weight of these pods was over 160 kg seriously affecting performance and maneuverability. In the photo an aircraft probably at Minsk with a gun pod visible under the port wing. **MiG-3** with additional armament was often referred to as **MiG-3P** and used in a ground attack role.

Mikoyan Gurievich MiG-3

Right and below:

Another **MiG-3** of 31 IAP captured at Kaunas, being examined by Germans. This aircraft is known also from other photos, as carring red no. "14" outlined on white.

Below:

Similarly marked **MiG-3**, but this time with no. "5", Kaunas airfield, summer 1941. I-16s in the background.

Left:
Some of the MiG-3s had bomb racks installed, as visible in this photo. The aircraft with yellow (?) tactical number "4".

Left:
Another **MiG-3** captured in Lithuania. A long list of the defects and other deficiencies of the new Soviet fighter caused the Finns to reject German offer to sell them some of the many captured **MiG-3** fighters.

Left and below:
MiG-3 bearing number "10" on its tail, captured in almost perfect condition. Note that tactical number is of stencil type.

Right:

Another wreck of a **MiG-3**. Note details of armament and lower part of the engine. The very large red star on the fuselage is very interesting.

Right:

One of the **MiG-3**s captured intact in the first days of the invasion. Many MiG's were abandoned at the airfield because only a handful of pilots could fly them. Others preferred to evacuate in I-16s and I-153s rather than difficult to fly MiGs. Only 61 pilots of different fighter regiments of 9 SAD completed training on the MiG, before German invasion. Fighter regiments of 9 SAD received 31 **MiG-1's** and 201 **MiG-3's** before the war.

Right:

German soldier in the cockpit of a **MiG-3**. Note that outer parts of the wing were painted in different paint, but the same colour, because they were made of wood.

Left and below:

Photos of **MiG-3** wrecks showing to advantage many interesting construction details.

Right:

This **MiG-3** of 15 SAD
was captured at the former
Polish airfield at Lwów.
                    Photo: Oesel.

Right:

Wreck of **MiG-3** captured
by Romanian troops in the
southern part of the front.
Photo taken at Beryozovka,
12 August 1941.

Right:

MiG-3 with radio outfit,
after forced landing.

Left and below:

MiG-3 in two-tone camouflage. First photo shows aircraft right after its capture, while the second one depicts this same aircraft after it lost some skin. Placed immediately under the cockpit is an inscription in Russian - "*For Motherland*".

Left:

Although of poor quality, this is a very interesting photo of **MiG-3** in German markings. Code 6+1 suggests there might be some connection to the German name for the aircraft: I-61.

Mikoyan
Gurievich **MiG-3**

Right:

Group of **MiG-3s** captured at Kaunas airfield, Lithuania.

Right:

Mig-3 captured in Lithuania. Note a very interestinf Ar-2 with small no. "2" on the rudder in the background.Right:

Right:

MiG-3 captured in Lithuania. Please note air intake below the exhaust and removed panels in front of the cockpit.

Right:

Concurrently with the **MiG-3**, the Russians started mass production of their second modern fighter the **LaGG-3**, and by June 1941 322 were completed. However, because of numerous faults the aircraft did not meet all of the requirements. Despite its problems the **LaGG-3** remained in production until September 1943. During the German invasion most of the LaGGs were in the Far East, and only the units of Moscow PVO had some (75), plus 2 in the Leningrad Military

District. **LaGG-3** first appeared in fighter units on the German - Russian front in the late summer and fall of 1941. This photo shows, a shot down **LaGG-3** of the first production series. Note duplicated tactical number – below the cockpit and on the tail.

Below:

Shot down **LaGG-3**, later series (note horn-balanced rudder). Winter camouflage.

Above:

Yak-1 was the most successful of the new "Frontal Fighters" introduced in 1941 (Yak-1, MiG-3 and LaGG-3). By 22 June 1941 only 451 had been built, but units of four Western Military Districts received no more than 105 Yaks and PVO units in Moscow another 95. In the photo, two Yaks from the first production series at the airfield captured by Germans.

Below:

In September 1941 the Yak-7 model entered production lines as a conversion of trainer aircraft Yak-7 UTI. In the photo Yak-7 captured by Germans. Photo was taken probably in summer 1942.

Reconnaissance aircraft R-5, captured at one of the air bases in Lithuania. These rather ancient biplanes were still in first line service with many units in the Western Military Districts.

Left:

On 22 June 1941 there were about 247 of them, both the **R-5** and the **R-ZET** aircraft in the units of the five Western Military Districts. In the photo, an **R-5** with TUR-8 machine-gun mount.

Left:

Inspection of an **R-5** after a forced landing somewhere near Kiev, August 1941. Shortly after the German attack the Russians started creating light bomber regiments equipped with **R-5** biplanes.

Polikarpov **R-5 (R-ZET)**

Right and below:

Old **R-5s** destroyed by the Germans in the southern part of the front line. Note the construction details.

Right:

This damaged **R-5** at one of the former Soviet air bases was photographed in winter 1941/42.

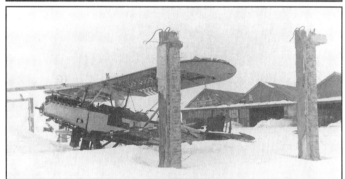

Right and next page:

Civil **R-ZET** with SSSR-F-121 code letters captured at Alytus airfield, Lithuania. Most civil aircraft were pressed into service after the Germans attacked Russia.

Left:
In the foreground, **R-ZET** destroyed by a bomb blast, in the background **R-5** and **UT-1**. Note that one of the R-5s has lighter colour wing tip and part of the fuselage, probably after repair.

Right:
Severely damaged **R-5** examined by German troops.

Right:

Designed by Aleksander Yakovlev, the **UT-1** was a very small and simple aircraft for advanced training. Used by many air divisions and regiments. Probably all UT-1s were painted in a similar way - silver overall with red trim. This photo was taken at Minsk.

Right:

Three **UT-1**s and a **Bf108** in front of the HQ building at one of the Soviet air bases.

Right:

UT-1 in the background with incomplete **I-16** in the front. Note the **I-16** engine details.

Left:
   UT-1 profile. Aircraft silver overall with red details.
   1,241 **UT-1** were built between 1937-1940.

Left:
   Gymnastic exercises at one of the airfields in Lithuania. **UT-1** employed as a body building equipment- the empty weight was only 429 kg.

Left:
   This **UT-1** without wheel covers was found at Lepel airfield, Belarus. Note other aircraft hidden in the bushes.

Left:
   Rest time at one of the captured Soviet airfields. Note the red star painted on upper surface of the wing, and a red outline to the horizontal stabiliser.

Right:

The **U-2**, designed by N. Polikarpov, entered production in 1929 and was still in production after WWII. From July 1944 it was known as the **Po-2**. More than 33,000 were built in many different versions. This photo, taken in summer 1941, shows **U-2** and an **I-153** at one of the Soviet airfields. Polikarpov's biplanes were rather rare at combat units, and were mostly used as liaison or auxiliary aircraft.

Right:

Another **U-2** left at one of bases captured by the Germans, this time with interesting stripe (yellow?) painted on the fuselage.

Right:

Forward part of the **U-2** fuselage. On the left, the wing of an **I-16** type 27 with ShVAK 20 mm gun can be seen, and standing on its nose is the wreck of another **U-2**.

Left:

Another **U-2** captured by Germans. In the background, **R-5** aircraft.

Left, below:

Two **U-2**s abandoned on the airfield ourskirt. Note tactical no. "5" and colour stripe on the tail, on the right aircraft.

Below:

Engineless **U-2** abandoned at the far end of the field. There is probably no. "3" on the rudder.

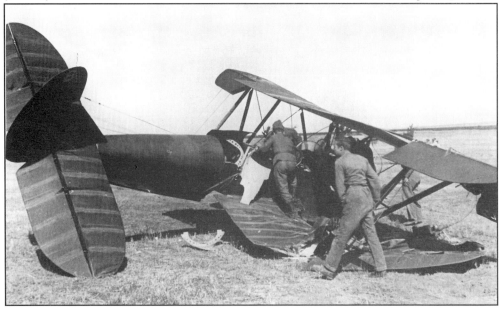

Above:
Shot down courier version of the **U-2**, known also as **U-2SP**.

Right:
German soldiers examining a special medical version of the **U-2** , **U-2S-2**.

Right:
In the fall of 1941 the Germans captured this camouflaged **U-2** with special wing medvac containers designed by G. I. Bakshayev.

Above:
Burning ski-equipped **U-2**.

Above and left:
Courier version of the **U-2** capable of carrying a pilot and two passengers. This force landed is in winter washable camouflage and on skis. Picture was taken at the end of 1941.

Above:

Designed by I. G. Neman, the **R-10** reconnaissance and light bomber was introduced in 1937, and by 1940 about 490 had been built. In the summer of 1941 they were rather rare in combat units of the VVS. On the day of the German attack only 57 were in the air units of the Western Military Districts. The aircraft seen in the photo was based in the Kiev Special Military District, and has a red lightning flash on the fin. Photo taken on 3 August 1941.

Below:

Collection of aircraft at an abandoned Russian airfield. Visible are four **R-10s**, one **I-153** and one **UTI-4**. All R-10s are silver overall, though the furthest one has a dark cowl. One of them with red tactical number "5".

Left:

Wrecks probably collected by the Germans at one of the air bases in the Western Military District. In the foreground is the wreck of an **R-10** in green camouflage, with faded light-coloured band on the fuselage. In the background is the nose of a **TB-3** bomber, with red star.

Left:

Another **R-10**, in a very patchy finish of silver and light grey. Note the MV 3 turret (ShKAS 7.62 machine gun is missing). The aircraft was also equipped with two ShKAS guns in wings and could carry up to 300 kg of bombs.

Right:

The first **Su-2** light bombers appeared in operational units in 1940. In June 1941 in the Western Special Military District there were 89 Su-2s, 99 in Kiev, and 21 in Odessa Military District. In the photo is Su-2 no. "4", but without engine or turret. **DB-3F** bomber in the background.

Right:

Su-2 in a hangar at one of the Soviet air bases. There were only two regiments equipped with the **Su-2** (earlier known as **BB-1**) in the Western Military District, 97 BBAP and 43 BBAP.

Right:

Wreck of an **Su-2**. Aircraft belonged to 211 BBAP, which in June 1941 was based at Kotovsk in the Odessa Military District. In the background is a **UTI-4.**

Probably the first **Il-2** ground attack aircraft were captured by the Germans, on 22 June 1941 at the Małyje Zwody airfield close to Brześć. 74 ShAP of 10 SAD was based there and was equipped with 8 Il-2s. Two days later the Germans captured the former Polish airfield Porubanek at Wilno, where they found the next Il-2 aircraft, this time of 57 SAD. Some of them were in very good condition. In the photo a pair of brand new Il-2s, captured at Wilno, can be seen. In the background is a Bf110 of ZG 26, Luftflotte 1.

Below:
One of the **Il-2**s seen in the previous photo. Note the armament: ShVAK 20 mm guns and RS-82 rocket rails, and aileron balance weight (projecting forward of the wing's leading edge), a characteristic feature of early Il-2s. By the end of June 1941 the Russians had produced 249 Il-2s in the GAZ-18 factory at Voronezh, but only 18 of them had been sent to units in the Western Military Districts, before the outbreak of war.

Right:

Il-2 left by the Soviets in June 1941, probably at one of the bases in the Western Military District. Tactical no. "5". Aircraft is probably of 74 ShAP or one of 57 SAD's regiments (Wilno).

Above:

Hungarian cavalry examining an **Il-2** shot down by AA, Ukraine, summer 1941.

Right and next page:

This **Il-2** was also captured by Hungarian troops, and shown to the public at an the exhibition of captured Soviet arma-ment in Budapest. Aircraft of the first production series, without armoured canopy.

Left and below:

Two shots of the same aircraft, captured by the Germans in late summer 1941. Note armament of the early **Il-2**, rear canopy with no armour, and the plain air inlet on the starboard wing's leading edge. Later aircraft had the characteristic external air filter in this place.

Right:

Il-2 of a later production series with armoured rear canopy section. Aircraft being examined by the Wermacht's top brass.

Above and right:

Wreck of an **Il-2**. During crash landings the rear part of the fuselage often broke off from the forward section, which was made from the armour plate forming a monocoque shell extending from the engine to the rear of the cockpit.

Photo: K.H. Münch

Left:

Another **Il-2** also broken in half. According to the official Soviet data about 1,500 Il-2s had been delivered to combat units by the end of 1941 - they lost more than 1,100 of them.

Left:

Early **Il-2** without engine left behind by the Russians at an airfield. Note the very interesting camouflage, probably painted at unit level. In the background another **Il-2** in dark green camouflage with a **Ju-52** about to land.

Below and next page:

This downed **Il-2** with yellow no. "9" on the rudder was also camouflaged. RS-82 rocket rails

under the wings are clearly visible. Rockets, together with guns, were often the only offensive weapons used, because **Il-2** pilots did not like to carry bombs. Loaded with bombs, **Il-2** was a monster to handle.

Right:

In the first months of the war hundreds of **Il-2**s were shot down by German fighters and Flak. The aircraft was rather slow, with a very limited rear field of vision.

Right:

Wing of an early **Il-2** (note aileron mass balance) found by the Germans at one of the VVS bases. Note four RS-82 rocket launchers. The rocket was not a very precise weapon, since the pilot had specialized sight for rocket aiming. Also the warhead itself was only a mere 0.36 kg.

Right:

Damaged **Il-2**, with an ammunition belt draped over the ShVAK gun barrel. This "flying tank", as it was called by Soviet propaganda, could carry only 400 kg of bombs (overload - 600 kg), far too little as for a modern attack aircraft.

Above:

Shot down **Il-2** with partially removed armament (lack of the left ShVAK gun). The end portion of the serial number (*211*) is still visible on the undercarriage nacelle .

Below:

A very interesting **Il-2** with tactical no. "6" or "8". Aircraft equipped with new 23 mm VYa-23 guns, which were installed on Il-2s from August 1941. Aircraft has triple exhausts, which was very rare. Also lack of aileron mass balances indicates this aircraft was produced after the begininig of the war. Not black painted area under the wings along the rockets rails.

Right:

The **SB** fast bomber was the mainstay of VVS air power. On the day of the German invasion, in western military districts they equipped 27 bomber regiments, a total of 1,646 SB bombers. This photo features an older version of the SB with M-100A engines, with flat radiators at the front of the nacelles. This aircraft has irregular, field applied, hand-painted camouflage over the original grey finish.

Right:

Captured **SB-2M-100A** also with field applied camouflage. This version of the SB reached a maximum speed of 424 km/h but could only carry 500 kg of bombs in the bomb bay. Additional bombs on racks under the wings decreased both the speed and the range of the bomber.

Right and next page:

Shot down **SB-2M-100A** in typical temporary camouflage. On the tail is the characteristic red "wing", different for each squadron of the regiment. Number of feathers in the wing, four in this case, designated the squadron number. Note the MV-2 turret introduced in later versions of the SB.

Left:

Destroyed **SB** of the same regiment. Only two "feathers", and different camouflage.

Left:

In the first days of the war **SB**s were shot down by German fighters in large numbers. This downed **SB-2M-100A** no. "8" has a "wing" with four feathers on the fin.

Right:

One more **SB** of the same regiment, left at the airfield and photographed by a German soldier in the late autumn of 1941. This aircraft has a "wing" with three feathers.

Right:

Front view of **SB** with M-100A engines. This version of Tupolev's SB was replaced by the SB with M-103 engines begining in 1941.

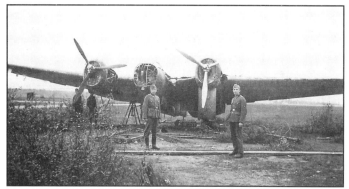

Right:

Shot down **SB** with tactical no. "4" in mid-December 1941. Aircraft in two tone camouflage with old rear gunner's position and old rear ShKAS TUR-9 mount.

Left:
   Undersurfaces of destroyed **SB**. Note ventral gun position. Movement from upper to lower position was very difficult, so the gunner was equipped with a special pedal which fired the lower gun. Effective aiming from this position was almost impossible.

Above:
   Nose of an **SB** showing the front turret for two ShKAS machine guns. These guns could move vertically, as well as horizontally - but by only within ± 15 degrees limit.

Right:
   Gun turret of a shot down **SB**. Note the ammunition feed, and damaged ShKAS machine gun.

Right:

German soldiers examining the cockpit of a shot down **SB** bomber.

Right and next page:

In September 1938 the Russians introduced into series production **SB** bombers with 960 HP M-103 engines (96 series). Thanks to the increased strength of its structure the aircraft could carry up to

1,500 kg of bombs in the bomb bay and under the wings. In the photo is an SB-2-M103 of 13 SBAP, shot down by Flak near Witebsk in August 1941. This aircraft still had nose radiators similar to the aircraft with M-100 engines.

Right:

One more **SB-2M-103**. This destroyed aircraft was found at one of the airfields in Lithuania.

Right:

SB bomber with **M-103** engines. Germans captured this **SB** at Mitau airfield, Latvia.

Right and next page:

In November 1939 the Russians started to bulid the **SB-2M-103**, 201 series, often mistakenly called **"SB-2bis"**. These aircraft received new ducted radiators and modified engine nacelles. Thanks to the drag reduction, maximum

speed was increased from 419 to 450 km/h. This series of the photos shows an **SB-2M-103**, 201 series, of 12 BAD captured at Vitebsk. The aircraft was painted green, as characteristic for the aircraft produced in 1939-41, and equipped with MV-3 rear gun turret and radio installation. Germans called the SB the "Martin Bomber", dating back to the common misidentification of SB bombers used by the Republicans during the Spanish Civil War.

Right:

One of 56 VVS aircraft captured at the former Polish airfield at Wilno. The aircraft was probably undergoing an overhaul, which could account for one missing engine. The new nacelle design considerably improved the pilot's field of view.

Right:

The same aircraft photographed from a different direction. On the rudder is the individual number "9".

Right:

Group of **SB** planes, probably of 40 SBAP, 6 SAD found at Mitau airfield. On the left, a light grey **SB-2M-103**, 201 series with ducted coolers and modified gun turret. On the right, silver SB-2M-103, 96 series with nose radiators, and red rudder trim.

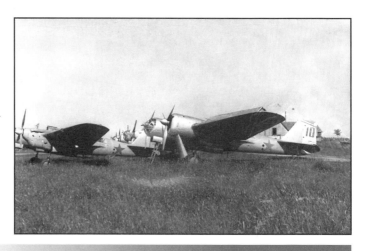

Left and below:

Two shots of abandoned **SB-2M-103** with new engine nacelles yet with the older type of gunner's position. Note TUR-9 machine gun mount and yellow tactical number "6" on the rudder.

Left and below:

Different **SB-2M-103** with individual yellow number "6". Aircraft modified by the unit to receive a new turret. Note the rails of the old fashioned gunner's canopy.

Right:

Similarly modified **SB**, but with gun position of different shape. Old gunner's canopy rails are still visible on the fuselage. Note the red identification trim on the fin. Aircraft probably captured at Mitau.

Right and below:

Two photos of an **SB** after a forced landing. This aircraft has an unusual two-tone camouflage painted over the original light grey overall colour.

SB-2M-103 with black "2" tactical number on the rudder, also after a forced landing. According to an order dated mid June 1941, the light grey overall colour was to be painted over with green patches. On the right, destroyed I-16 with white "9" on the tail.

Left:
  SB destroyed during a forced landing near Witebsk in July 1941.

Left and next page:
  Light grey **SB-2M-103** with non-standard camouflage painted on upper surfaces, found by the Germans at a Soviet airfield. Tactical no. "10" on the rudder in red. Dorsal gunner's position is of the older version.

Right:

Wreck of **SB** left by the Russians during their retreat. Note two-colour upper surface camouflage - best seen behind the cockpit and on the tail.

Right:

Light grey **SB** modified to carry 10 RS-132 rocket rails, quite rare on SBs. Aircraft in the photo was the last version of **SB-2M-103** to have the ventral gun position. Aircraft of one of the 57 SAD regiments, captured on 24 June 1941 at Wilno airfield.

Left and below:

Very poor quality, but extremely interesting photos of light grey **SB** with unusual markings. Instead of the usual number, the rudder bears Cyrillic letter "**E**". Rudder with colour trim, probably in squadron colour. Gun position with TUR-9 mount is visible.

Below:

SB with M-103 engines, nosed over on during crash landing. Aircraft is light grey overall with red (?) tactical no. "5" on the rudder.

Right:

Photo taken on 3 July 1941 showing red stars on an **SB**'s spinners. These could be an element of the official marking scheme, or just an individual decoration. Note propeller colours.

Right:

This **SB-2M-103** was completely destroyed by a direct hit from a small bomb or due to self-destruction by the Russians. Note that this aircraft has radio equipment.

Right and next page:

Two photos of the aircraft from the same production series. Of all **SB** bombers available at the western border, 175 were unserviceable - almost 11.5% of the total number.

Left:
This **SB-2M-103** was captured by Slovak troops on the southern part of the front and received Slovak markings on the wings and on the tail. In the photo, taken in the summer of 1941, the aircraft has crashed at the former Polish airfield Skniłów at Lwów.

Left:
Forced landing of SB with radio installation. Spinners are probably red.

Above:

Wreck of **SB** with unit-applied camouflage. Note the small star painted on the rudder and no. "12". Gunner's canopy frame of the older type in the foreground.

Below:

In 1938 a trainer version of the **SB** bomber entered production - the **USB**. USBs were used at combat units to speed up conversion to the **SB**. **USB** was different from the standard **SB** only in the nose section, with instructor's cockpit replacing the turret. This modification could be easy performed on a regular SB. About 500-600 **USB** were built, but only a few as a brand new aircraft. Most were modified SBs with new nose sections delivered from the factory.

The **USB** with dark green upper surfaces and a unit-fitted new nose in natural metal, captured on 28 June 1941 at Minsk as seen in the photo.

Left:
The same aircraft, showing stars on upper surfaces. **I-153** wrecks in the background.

Left, below:
Remains of a **USB** destroyed at Mołodeczno airfield. In the middle, the instructor's cockpit, on the left, part of the wing with no. "6" painted underneath.

Below:
This silver **USB** with dark green nose has a stylised tactical no. "4" and rudder trim, probably in black. Note that fuselage star is of plain type, but wing stars have black outlines. Nose of an early **MiG-3** in the foreground.

The **Ar-2,** dive bomber was a development of the **SB**. **Ar-2** had different nose, new engines, and shorter wingspan. The new bomber also had a new tail.

Ar-2 was produced from 1940 to 1941 in Zavod no. 22 factory. About 220 (according to different sources 250) were built. On the day of the German invasion each of western military districts had 22-23 **Ar-2** aircraft - 115 of them altogether. In the photo is an **Ar-2** captured by Germans at an airfield of the Baltic Special Military District. Note redesigned engine nacelles. Thanks to the new radiators repositioned into wings and better engines (M-105 with 1050 HP) the **Ar-2** could reach the speed of 475 km/h.

Two photos of **Ar-2** with tactical no. "2" captured almost intact. **Bf109** in the background suggests the photo was taken in July, in the northern part of the Eastern front.

Left:
   Ar-2 could carry up to 1,500 kg of bombs in the bomb bay and under wings. Note underwing airbrakes.

Right:

Ar-2 of one of the regiments equipped with SB bombers, with tactical no. "4". Note the spherical nose turret for ShKAS machine gun, similar in shape to that of He 111.

Right:

Rear view of one of the Ar-2s of 132 SBAP, 45 SAD captured at Kirovograd. Note red star on the wing and no. "7" on the rudder.

Right:

3/4 rear view of Ar-2.

Right:

Damaged, probably hit by 37 mm Flak, Ar-2 after a forced landing. Very soon most of the Ar-2s were lost in combat. For example in 33 SBAP of 19 BAD, Kiev Military District, on 22 June 1941 there were 23 Ar-2s but by 11 July there were only four left - with just two in flyable condition.

Yak-2 photographed on 20 July 1941 after a forced landing close to Demitov, in the northern part of the front. **Yak-2** was a very rare bird in the VVS, with only 201 of the Yak-2/Yak-4 series built. Some of them were delivered to the units of Western Special Military District and Kiev Special Military District.

Right and below:

Two more photos of the same aircraft.

Right :

Wreck of a **Yak-2** lying close to the road. There were only 12 Yak-2s in the Western Special Military District and about 80 in the Kiev Special Military District on 22 June 1941. The aircraft were used as light bombers and for reconnaissance duties. Note exhaust stacks of M-103 engines arranged horizontally (buried in the wing) and aerial mast on the starboard engine nacelle.

Left:

The **Yak-4** had a new M-105 engines, increasing its maximum speed to 533 km/h, but this aircraft retained the Yak-2's low stability, inadequate firepower and lack of durability.

Left and below:

Two shots of the same **Yak-4**. Note details distinquishing it from the **Yak-2**: dual main wheels, air intake under the spinner (no side intakes on the cowling) and entirely exposed exhaust pipes over the wing. Under the port wing is a bomb rack.

Yakovlev **Yak-2, Yak-4**

Right:

Luftwaffe personnel examining a **Yak-4** abandoned close to a forest at one of the Kiev Special Military District airfields. On the day of the German invasion only 16 Yak-4s were in units of the Western Special Military District and about 20 in units of the Kiev Special Military District.

Right and below:

Yak-4 after a forced landing somewhere in the southern part of the front. Note construction details.

Pe-2 dive bomber captured at Mitau airfield. The Pe-2 was a modern and successful light bomber, but by 22 June 1941 only 205 had been delivered to units on the German - Russian border. Most of them were in the Kiev and Western Special Military Districts.

Left:

Early **Pe-2**. Airbrakes under the wings are easily visible. Aircraft could carry 600 kg of bombs or 1,000 kg in overload. First production machines were armed with four ShKAS 7.62 mm machine guns: 2 in the nose (removed from the aircraft in the photo), one behind the cockpit mounted on a TSS-1 mount, and one in the ventral position under the fuselage on a MW-2 mount. From May 1941 the ventral gun and the starboard nose gun were replaced by Beresin 12.7 mm machine guns.

Left:

Pe-2 shot down by Flak, enters its final dive.

Right:

Wreck of shot-down **Pe-2**. There were not enough Pe-2s available in the early stages of the war, and crews were not trained to use the aircraft to its full potential. Many Pe-2s were destroyed on the ground, many others were shot down by German pilots due to their air superiority.

Right:

Early **Pe-2** shot down in summer 1941, being examined by German soldiers.

Right and next page:

Evidently the Russians did not have enough time to repair this **Pe-2**, and abandoned it fleeing the advancing Germans. Note the interesting camouflage pattern, and construction details.

Left and below:

This brand new **Pe-2**, together with many other VVS aircraft, was captured by the Germans. Greenhouse nose was modified in later Pe-2s, losing many of the glazed panels.

DB-3 and **DB-3F** aircraft were the main elements of VVS strategic air power (DBA), commanded directly by the Commander in Chief. In the west part of the USSR there were four air corps and one independent air division, equipped with a total of 1,332 aircraft including 1,122 DB-3/DB-3F. In the photos is an early DB-3, from 1937 or 1938 production batch, captured at Mitau airfield. Aircraft probably of 1 BAK, based in area of Leningrad Military District.

Right:

DB-3 after forced landing in German territory. Aircraft could carry about 1,000 kg of bombs in fuselage. Range with 1,000 kg bomb load was 3,100 km, but with 1,500 kg of bombs in the bomb's bay and under the wings its range, was much limited. Aircraft in the photo was equipped with a radio, and had one of the spinners painted.

Left:

DB-3 with damaged nose after collision. Silver overall, but with spinners in squadron colour. Photo was taken at Porchov (east of Pskov) in August 1941. Aircraft probably of 40 or 51 DBAD based in the Leningrad Military District.

Left:

One of 1,528 **DB-3**s produced, after a forced landing in the Novorzhev area. Interesting camouflage sample, green patches brushed over silver background. Red spinners.

DB-3M of the Finnish Air Force at an exhibition of captured Russian equipment in Finland. The red star insignia have been temporarily reapplied for this purpose. The Finns used several captured DB-3s operationally.

Above:

On the night of 7/8 August 1941 the Russians made their first air raids over Berlin. **DB-3T** bombers (torpedo version of DB-3) of 1 MTAP Red Banner Air Fleet flew from Kagul Base at Ösel island, where the distance to Berlin was only 890 km. Mostly a propaganda action, raids continued for a month and cost the Russians 9 crews and 20 aircraft. During the last raid on 4/5 September 1941, German Flak shot down one of two DB-3s that have been spotted. In the photo is the wing of a shot down DB-3T of 1 MTAP. Aircraft serial no. 391114 flown by Ltn. Milgunov.

Above and below:

In mid 1940 long-range bomber units started to receive a new version of the **DB-3** - the **DB-3F**. These featured a new greenhouse nose, new engines (M-88) and modified wings. All this changes resulted in improved bomb load and increased maximum speed (up to 422 km/h). In the photo a brand new, unpainted DB-3F can be seen. Production DB-3Fs were usually painted with dark green uppersurfaces and light blue undersurfaces. This aircraft was captured at Bobruisk. Tactical no. "11" on the rudder means this aircraft belonged to one of the regiments of 3 BAK.

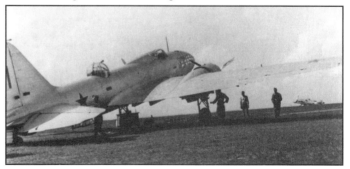

Left:

In the first days of the war the Russians threw medium bombers against German motorised divisions, which were pouring into Soviet territory. Used as a tactical bomber the **DB-3**s suffered heavy losses. In the photo, taken on 27 June 1941, the remains of a **DB-3F** shot down in Belarus. Tactical no. "9" on the rudder, and old version of the rear turret as used on the **DB-3**.

Left and below:

This **DB-3F** destroyed on the ground by SD-2 bombs had tactical no. "10". Note new version of the upper turret of MV-3 type.

Right:

German soldiers are looking for souvenirs in the wreck of a **DB-3F**. Photo was taken on 14 July 1941.

Right:

DB-3F from a later series, with different style engine air intakes in wing leading edges. Aircraft abandoned by the Russians at an auxiliary airfield.

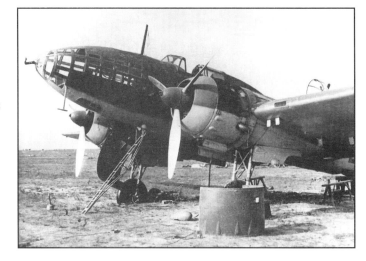

Right:

From March 1942 **DB-3F** was designated Ilyushin **Il-4**, and was produced until the end of 1945. 5,256 were built. In the photo is an aircraft which belonged to one of the air divisions of 3 BAK, captured at the end of June 1941 at Borisov airfield, Belarus.

Left and below:

The same aircraft, moved to the remote part of the airfield. Note its rather high tactical no. "72" and stripped down elevators. Also note **I-153** "3" and various German aircraft.

Left:

Shot down **DB-3F** after a forced landing. **DB-3F** was the most expensive VVS aircraft because of its all metal construction. Note the colour of the spinner, and the way the MV-3 turret opened.

Right:

This broken **DB-3F** was awaiting transportation to a repair depot. Railways destroyed by German bombs made that impossible.

Right, below:

On 3 October 1941 German Second Panzer Army captured Orel. At Orel's airfield German tank crews found **DB-3**F aircraft of, among others, 100 DBAP, 35 DBAD, 2 BAK. This bomber has a small star on the fin and tactical number "8".

Below:

Repair workshop in Orel, October 1941. In the foreground, wreck of a **DB-3F** cannibalised for spare parts or prepared for a general overhaul, after suffering heavy damage. In the background, dark green **DB-3.**

PS-84 (from September 1942 known as Lisunov **Li-2**) was a licence-built DC-3 with Russian ASh-63IR engines. The aircraft was more than 400 kg heavier than DC-3, and inferior in performance. In the photos a **PS-84** shot down in autumn 1941, probably in the Vyazma area, is visible. Note gun turret on the fuselage, two colour camouflage and tactical number "926" painted in a dark colour.

Older version of the **TB-3** with M-17 engines, left in the field, August 1941. These ancient bombers were still used in four front-line regiments of DBA: 7TBAP of 40 DBAD, 3 TBAP of 52 DBAD, 1 TBAP of 42 DBAD and 14 TBAP of 18 DBAD; a total of 201 aircraft. Photo shows how big the **TB-3** actually was! Tactical number "3" with white outline.

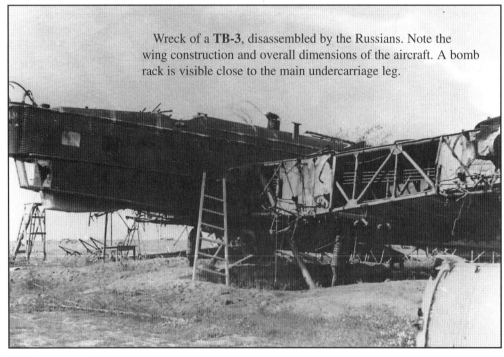

Wreck of a **TB-3**, disassembled by the Russians. Note the wing construction and overall dimensions of the aircraft. A bomb rack is visible close to the main undercarriage leg.

Above:

One of the very few **TB-3 4 M-17** with two colour camouflage, and red stars on engines and nose. This aircraft, probably of 3 TBAP, was captured in the central part of the front. Between the engines two Der-13 bomb racks are visible. Each of the Der-13 bomb racks could carry one 250 kg bomb; 28 bombs of 50 to 100 kg could be carried in the bomb bay in the fuselage where Der-9 bomb rack was installed. Bomb load of this "Dinosaur Bomber" was about 4,000 kg. However, the maximum speed was only 197 km/h.

Left:

Close up view of the same aircraft. Note M-17 engine nacelles, and tandem wheels of the main undercarriage.

Right and below:

Two more shots of the same **TB-3** taken much later. For many months this bomber was a main attraction for German soldiers based in that area. From other published photos of this **TB-3** it is know that the aircraft had a red tactical number "6" with white outline on the rudder.

Right and next page:

Two photos showing a **TB-3 4 M-17** destroyed on the ground.

In June 1941 some **TB-3**s of the heavy bombers regiments were used for daylight, almost suicidal attacks against fast moving German armoured columns. In the photo German soldiers are examining the wreck of a shot down **TB-3 4 M-17**.

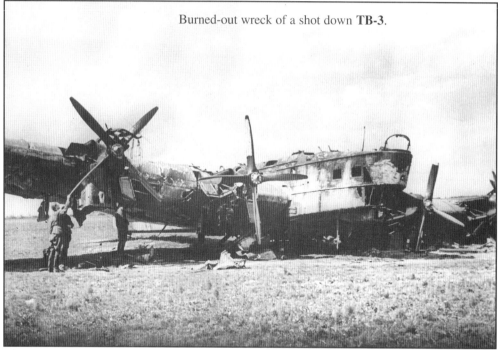

Burned-out wreck of a shot down **TB-3**.

Below:

TB-3 of the later series with M-34R engines, capable of reaching 288 km/h. Aircraft was equipped with four Der-15 bomb racks, and four Der-16 under the fuselage. Der-15 could carry 250-500 kg bombs and Der-16 - 1000 kg bombs. Under the wings were Der-13 bomb racks for 250 kg bombs.

Above and below:

Two shots of the same aircraft, left at Soltsy between Pskov and Novogorod. Aircraft belonged to 7 TBAP of 40 DBAD, based in the Leningrad Military District.

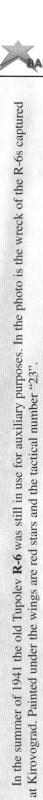

In the summer of 1941 the old Tupolev **R-6** was still in use for auxiliary purposes. In the photo is the wreck of the R-6s captured at Kirovograd. Painted under the wings are red stars and the tactical number "23".

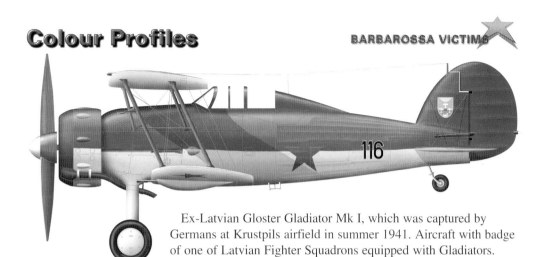

Ex-Latvian Gloster Gladiator Mk I, which was captured by Germans at Krustpils airfield in summer 1941. Aircraft with badge of one of Latvian Fighter Squadrons equipped with Gladiators. Note Soviet red star insignia and black Latvian serial number "116" with white outline.

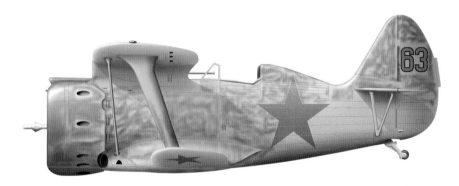

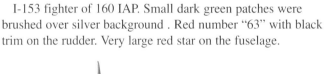

I-153 fighter of 160 IAP. Small dark green patches were brushed over silver background . Red number "63" with black trim on the rudder. Very large red star on the fuselage.

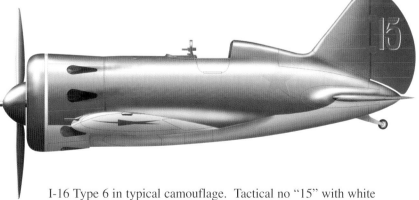

I-16 Type 6 in typical camouflage. Tactical no "15" with white shadow on the rudder.

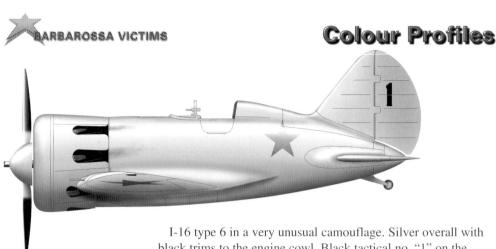

I-16 type 6 in a very unusual camouflage. Silver overall with black trims to the engine cowl. Black tactical no. "1" on the rudder.

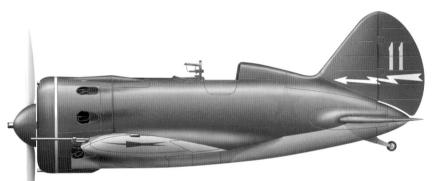

I-16 type 27 with ShVAK 20 mm guns in the wings and two ShKAS machine guns over the engine. Aircraft is probably of one of the 43 IAD regiments - 161, 162 or 163 IAP. Yellow tactical no. "11" with white lighting below.

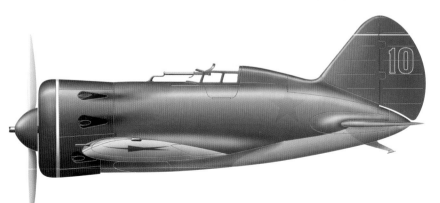

I-16 Type 5 with red fin tip and red "10" with white outline. Aircraft captured in Siauliai Air Base.

Colour Profiles

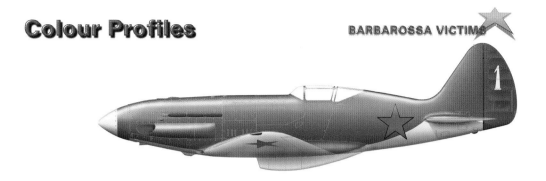

MiG-3 captured at Lithuania with unusual, crudely applied
tactical no "1", probably in yellow.

UT-1 trainer.
Aircraft silver overall with red details, without any numbers.

R-5, captured by Germans at one of the air bases in Lithuania.
Dark Green upper surfaces with Light Blue undersurfaces.

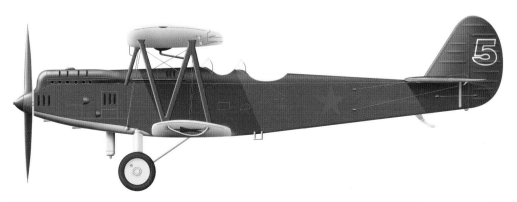

Yak-2, Dark Green uppersurfaces and Light Blue undersurfaces.

Il-2 of 57 SAD captured at former Polish airfield Porubanek at Wilno, with tactical no "4".

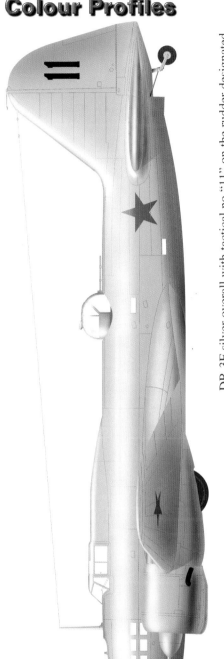

DB-3F silver overall with tactical no "11" on the rudder designated that aircraft belonging to one of the regiments of 3 BAK.

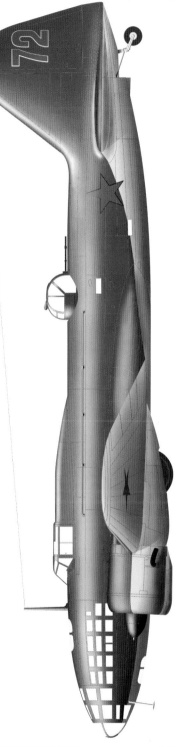

DB-3F of an air division of 3 BAK captured by the Germans at the end of June 1941 at Borisov airfield, Belarus. Dark Green upper surfaces and Light Blue under surfaces.

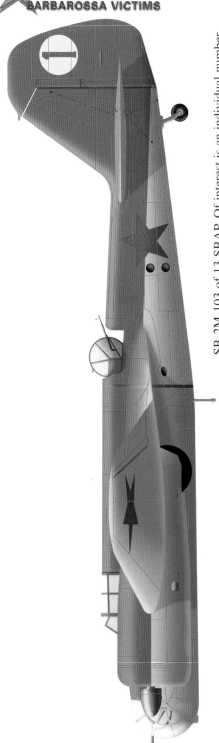

SB-2M-103 of 13 SBAP. Of interest is an individual number "1" in the circle on the fin.. Aircraft still has nose radiators similar to these fitted with M-100 engines.

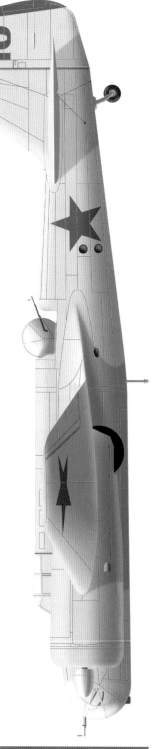

Silver SB-2M-103, 96 series with nose radiators and red rudder trim, probably of 40 SBAP, 6 SAD found by Germans at Mitau airfield.

Colour Profiles

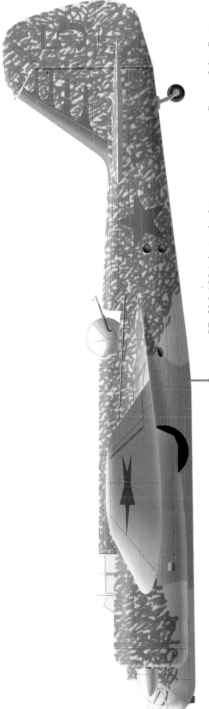

SB-2M-100A in typical temporary camouflage of the first weeks of the war. On the tail characteristic red "wing", different for each squadron of the regiment.

SB-2M-103 with fitted at the unit level gun turret and yellow tactical number "6" on the rudder. Aircraft light grey overall.

SB with M-100A engines, with flat radiators at the front of the nacelles. This aircraft has irregular, field applied, hand-painted camouflage over the original grey finish.

Silver overall, USB with dark green nose has odd-shaped tactical no "4" on the rudder and very interesting marking on the fin, probably in red. Stars on the fuselage are without trim, but wing stars are outlined in black .

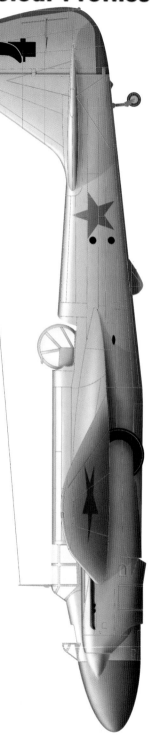